THE ROLE OF THE OFFICE OF STRATEGIC SERVICES
IN OPERATION TORCH

ABSTRACT

THE ROLE OF THE OFFICE OF STRATEGIC SERVICES IN OPERATION TORCH, by Major Thomas W. Dorrel, Jr. 103 pages.

This thesis evaluates the role of Allied strategic and operational intelligence in conjunction with Department of State actions in French North Africa from 1940 through the invasion, Operation TORCH, November 8, 1942. The primary focus is to evaluate whether or not the OSS collected the required intelligence information as their accounts have stated. This paper also looks at the operational requirements of advance force operations to determine if the OSS was successful in accomplishing the required tasks for the operational planning and execution of Operation TORCH. The final analysis reveals that the OSS was successful in answering most of the information requirements, but only with the help of other Allied intelligence collection agencies.

ACKNOWLEDGMENTS

I would like to thank my family for the time and consideration to pursue my interest in this subject. I would also like to acknowledge those men and women who set out into unknown territory to find information necessary for the Allies to fight the Axis. These first steps made in French North Africa set the stage in Europe for how the Allies would fight the war.

TABLE OF CONTENTS

ACRONYMS

AF	Advance Force
AFO	Advance Force Operations
COI	The Office of the Coordinator of Information
ETO	European Theater of Operations
FBI	Federal Bureau of Investigation
JIC	Joint Intelligence Sub-Committee (US & UK)
JCS	Joint Chiefs of Staff (US)
MID	Military Intelligence Division (US Army)
ONI	Office of Naval Intelligence (US)
OSS	The Office of Strategic Services
SOE	Special Operations Executive (UK)

TIMELINE

1939

- September 1: Germany invades Poland

1940

- May 1: Germany invades France

- June 16: Marshal Pétain becomes French Prime Minister

- June 18: Pétain sues for peace with Germany

- June 21: William Stephenson "Intrepid" arrives in America

- June 22: France signs an armistice with Germany creating occupied and unoccupied (Vichy) France

- June 25: German-French Armistice is in effect

- July 3: Robert D. Murphy becomes Charges d'affaires to Vichy France

- July 3: British Navy attacks French Fleet at various ports in order to deny German access to the vessels

- July 5: British and Vichy French Government break all relations

- July 14: Colonel William Donovan departs for Great Britain

- July: Commander Roscoe H. Hillenkoetter returns from survey of French North Africa

- September: Mr. Murphy is recalled to Washington to receive instructions from President Roosevelt on further diplomatic actions with the French government in North Africa

- November: President Roosevelt calls Colonel Donovan to Washington to discuss with him a fact-finding trip throughout the Mediterranean area

- December 6: Colonel Donovan departs for the Mediterranean stopping in England first

- December 18: Mr. Murphy departs Vichy, France for Algiers, Algeria

1941

- January 5: Mr. Murphy completes his assessment of French North Africa and returns to Washington

- February 12: German General Erwin Rommel arrives in Tripoli, North Africa

- February 14: First units of German Afrika Korps arrive in North Africa

- February 21: The Weygand-Murphy Accord is signed allowing economic support to Vichy France, primarily French North Africa

- March 18: Colonel Donovan returns to the United States from the Mediterranean Area

- April: Twelve vice-consuls selected for duty in French North Africa

- May 1: Major "Rygor" Slowikowski receives notice from London to plan for establishment of clandestine intelligence service in French North Africa

- June 10: First group of the vice-consuls arrive in Algiers

  June 22: Germany attacks the Soviet Union

- July 11: The Office of the Coordinator of Information is established

- July 15: The remainder of the vice-consuls arrives in Algiers, Algeria

- July 22: Major "Rygor" arrives in Algiers

- July 25: Major "Rygor" receives first messages to London from Algiers

- August 1 and 13: Major "Rygor" transmits first detailed notes on Military and

Infrastructure to London

- October: Colonel Donovan instructed to merge 'K' Division of the ONI with COI

- December 7: Japanese attack Pearl Harbor

- December 8: The United States declares war on Japan

- December 11: Germany declares war on the United States

- December 22 – January 14, 1942 Arcadia Conference between President Roosevelt and Prime Minister Churchill is conducted. This establishes the Europe first strategy for the war and provides a first look at North Africa option for action against the Axis.

1942

- January 3: Lieutenant Colonel (USMCR) William Eddy departs for Tangiers to establish COI outpost and begin operational control of the vice-consuls

- January 6: Lieutenant Colonel Eddy tells the vice-consuls to send all intelligence packages to him unsealed

- January 9: The vice-consuls in Algiers inform Major "Rygor" to deliver his intelligence unsealed, in accordance with Lieutenant Colonel Eddy's instructions

- May 22: Lieutenant Colonel Eddy departs for Washington D.C. to discuss French North Africa with Colonel Donovan and members of the Joint Chiefs

- June 13: The Office of Coordinator of Information is officially changed to the Office of Strategic Services and placed under the Joint Chiefs of Staff for command and control

- June 24: Lieutenant General Dwight Eisenhower arrives in London

- June: OSS clandestine radio network in French North Africa is established

- July 24: Planning for Operation TORCH began officially by the Combined Joint Chiefs after agreement by President Roosevelt and Prime Minister Churchill

- August 31: Mr. Murphy departs for Washington D.C. for briefings with President Roosevelt and Joint Chiefs on current situation in French North Africa

- September 4: President Roosevelt tells Mr. Murphy the operational plans for the invasion of French North Africa at Hyde Park

- September 11: Lieutenant Colonel Eddy briefs the Joint Chiefs on the current intelligence and insurgency support in French North Africa

- September 14: Mr. Murphy departs for England to brief Lieutenant General Eisenhower on the current situation in French North Africa

- September 15: Two French Moroccans arrive in England for harbor navigational support during the invasion

- October: Mr. Murphy and Lieutenant Colonel Eddy return to French North Africa and begin preparations for the invasion

- October 22-25: Major General Brian Clark arrives in Algeria for talks with Brigadier General Mast

- October 23: British Eighth Army attacks General Rommel's Afrika Korps at El Alamein

- November 1: Operation SUPERCHARGE begins in Libya as the British break through the Axis lines at El Alamein

- November 4: Major "Rygor" is told the date of the invasion by vice-consul John Knox

- November 8 0001: Resistance forces begin their role in preparation for the Allied

- November 8 0500: Allied forces begin the invasion at four major ports and two airfields

- November 11: Final agreements made with Vichy France and Marshal Pétain as to the conditions of the French Surrender to the Allies in French North Africa

- November 12: Germany occupies the French Unoccupied Territory and the French Navy scuttles their ships in Toulouse, France

CHAPTER 1

INTRODUCTION

Before World War II, America's use of covert, or shadow, warfare was limited. There had been spies in the Revolutionary and Civil War's, among others, but America intelligence services were so much inferior to those of the world's other great powers that one senior Foreign Service officer observed: 'Our Intelligence organization in 1940 was primitive and inadequate…operating strictly in the tradition of the Spanish-American War.'
>   - Patrick K. O'Donnell, *Operatives, Spies, and Saboteurs:*
>   *The Unknown Story of the Men and Women of World War*
>   *II's OSS.*[1]

Officially, the planning for Operation TORCH, the Allied invasion of French North Africa, started on July 24, 1942, when President Franklin D. Roosevelt agreed with the British Prime Minister Winston S. Churchill and his planners to commit United States forces to the invasion of French North Africa before the year's end. They agreed to this course of action in order to open a second front against the Germans in order to relieve pressure on the British Eighth Army fighting in Libya and western Egypt and the Soviet Union fighting on their western front. However, Allied intelligence collection in French North Africa began for the Americans in December 1940 and for the British in July 1941 through their Polish led intelligence agency, Agency Africa. As can be imagined, the planning for the longest distance amphibious invasion of World War II did not just occur in three months. It was through a dedicated team of United States intelligence amateurs, key Polish officers, and their French recruits, who provided the necessary intelligence required by advance force operations doctrine for the success of the invasion over the course of the preceding eighteen months.

There have been many scholars and critics of the Office of Strategic Services (OSS) and its role in Operation TORCH. These critics have made accusations about the skills and accomplishments of the men who volunteered to go to French North Africa and gather intelligence prior to the Allied invasion. Yet as these men have pointed out, they were rank amateurs, hoping to get it right. While this was not exactly a confidence builder in Allied intelligence, it was the truth. This is a story of ingenuity and fumbles, but ultimately, like many spy stories of World War II, it was an operational success because all of the intended objectives were met. Sadly, approximately 1,400 American and British soldiers and sailors died during the three days of fighting before the Allies and the French agreed to final terms.

Advance force operations and intelligence collection are never glorious or glamorous, yet they are highly necessary to all echelons of national power. President Franklin Roosevelt and Prime Minister Winston Churchill understood this, as did Colonel William Donovan, the creator and director of the Office of the Coordinator of Information (COI) (later redesignated as the OSS). The actions of the men and women who conduct these operations are by necessity, quiet and unassuming. The best advance force operation is the one never officially acknowledged. This was not completely the case in French North Africa, but as will be discussed, the elements of strategic and operational intelligence collection are present and the requirements for advance force operations was greatly explored and developed.

The invasion of French North Africa was the OSS's first attempt to conduct advance force operations. This paper will focus on the primary question: Did a fledgling American intelligence organization, the Office of Coordinator of Intelligence (later the

OSS), accomplish all of the required advance force operation tasks as outlined in Department of Defense Joint Publication 3-02.1 *Joint Tactics, Techniques, and Procedures for Landing Force Operations* to ensure the success of the Allied invasion of French North Africa? Ultimately, the OSS succeeded in providing the necessary information to the planning and execution of the operation. However, they were successful because of a combined effort between several groups to ensure the success of the Allies.

The International Stage

On November 8, 1942, United States Army and Navy forces conducted their first allied amphibious assault in the European Theater of War during World War II, against France, a declared neutral country and America's oldest international friend. However, the invasion was the final act in a drama for information, which had begun nearly two years earlier by a few men conducting intelligence collection and advance force operations. These men, initially led by a United States Department of State representative, Robert D. Murphy, laid the framework for operations in North Africa prior to the invasion.

The United States entered into a war for which only a few departments in the government had prepared for. The years of isolation had taken their toll on the government and more importantly on the intelligence services of the United States. The United States intelligence apparatus was far behind most European countries in capability, staffing, and understanding of events on the world stage. Yet, the intelligence collection, analysis and support by the OSS for the planning, preparation and execution of Operation TORCH was to be the proof of concept for the development and use of a strategic and operational intelligence organization in the United States for the rest of World War II and long after the war was complete.

Germany

Germany had begun its military expansion in September 1939 against Poland, the ripple effect felt across Europe, and the world was shattering. Hitler had moved quickly diplomatically and his army had moved decisively into Poland, where the Soviets assisted him by their occupation of the eastern half of Poland. In May 1940, Germany attacked again, this time westward through Belgium and the Netherlands and into France. Within six weeks, the German Army marched into Paris and defeated the Third Republic under President Albert Lebrun. On June 18, 1940, just two days after Marshal Pétain took control of the French government, he sued for peace with Hitler, in order to save his country.

The Germans and French signed the Armistice on June 22, 1940, and it went into effect on June 25. The terms of the Armistice created two French Governments. One was a German puppet government in Vichy, France under Marshal Pétain. The second, a semi-independent colonial French Africa governed initially by General Maxime Weygand, French Hero of World War I and the last commanding general of French Forces days before their defeat by the Germans in June. A combined German-Italian Armistice Commission oversaw this colonial government; however, German troops themselves did not occupy the French Colonies. General Charles de Gaulle, a French declared renegade, established a third government in London named Free France, which the British government recognized on June 28, 1940.

As a part of the Armistice, the Germans left most of the French Navy intact and allowed an army of 120,000 troops and equipment to remain in North Africa for colonial defense only. In 1940-1941, Germany, as a part of the Armistice, only wanted the rubber latex, food supplies, and oil/gasoline reserves from the French North African colonies for their war efforts.

Rumors were rampant within unoccupied France and the African colonies, of Germany's intentions to invade within the next year. However, German career diplomat Theodor Auer assured Mr. Murphy that this was not one of Hitler's declared intentions for 1941. As Murphy was negotiating his economic agreement with General Weygand, Auer told Murphy that he had "persuaded the Nazi Foreign Office to replace the Italians on the Armistice Commission and soon would have enough Germans here to do that job properly. But, he said he could not stir up much real interest in Berlin."[2] These comments were of importance to Murphy and Weygand who based all of the proposals made as a part of the economic accord on the assumption and rumors that Germany would invade the unoccupied area of France and French North Africa within the year. Germany's suspected plans and ambitions drove the French leadership to make concessions with the Americans. It also allowed other options to be presented for economic and material support by the Allies, but again primarily from the Americans.

However, on February 12, 1941, General Erwin Rommel arrived in Tripoli, North Africa and two days later, the lead elements of his Afrika Korps arrived. His mission was to destroy the British Eighth Army in Egypt and secure the Suez Canal, thereby closing the British transit route to India and the Mediterranean Sea from Allied use. By the spring of 1942, Rommel has almost completed his mission by routing the British Eighth

Army, pushing eastward to positions near Cairo, Egypt.

Five months after Rommel initiated operations in Libya and Egypt against the

British, the Eastern Front erupted as Germany on June 22, 1941, invaded its recent ally,

the Soviet Union. German successes against the Soviet Red Army into late December of

1941, forced Premier Joseph Stalin to send Foreign Minister Vyacheslav Molotov to meet

with President Roosevelt and Prime Minister Churchill and request opening a second

front against Germany to relieve his forces. Because of Hitler's attack eastward into the

Soviet Union and with Rommel's success in Libya and Egypt against the British Eighth

Army, and insufficient strength in man and material for an assault into France, the Allies

had little choice but to look to French North Africa as the second front.

Great Britain

In 1909, the British created a permanent and publicly funded spy service, which

by 1941 had established a strong and disciplined intelligence force capable of providing

operational level intelligence and analysis. As early as the fall of 1939, Churchill, then

the British First Lord of the Admiralty, realized he had sensitive information to pass to

his greatest potential ally, the United States, but he needed to ensure that the information

was handled carefully so as not to reveal or endanger the source of the intelligence.

Churchill was also looking at a way to present this information to the senior leaders in the

United States government as objectively and precise as possible. In order to begin

sharing this information, Churchill worked to influence President Roosevelt on creating

an intelligence service for the United States. In late 1939 and early 1940, Churchill first

sent Admiral John H. Godfrey, then Director of British Naval Intelligence, and

Commander Ian Fleming to review carefully the state of American intelligence services. They returned to London and reported to the Prime Minister that the United States was not ready to receive and safeguard the type of intelligence information the British were willing to provide. President Roosevelt desired as much intelligence and operational information as he could receive to begin subtlety improving the readiness of the United States against fighting Germany; however, the United States was still a declared neutral country and could not readily act on any of this information, operationally and overtly.

Later in 1940, Churchill sent Sir William "Intrepid" Stephenson, a Canadian-born millionaire industrialist to the United States. His mission was to help organize an American intelligence apparatus to share intelligence information. He operated out of a suite in Rockefeller Center in New York under the title British Passports Control Officer. After Pearl Harbor and the United States entry into World War II, he became the British Security Coordinator for the Western Hemisphere.

Prime Minister Churchill knew Donovan had a close ear to Roosevelt and a good grasp of the need for a national intelligence organization. Because of this, he instructed Stephenson to foster a working relationship with Colonel William Donovan. This relationship developed quickly between Stephenson and Donovan. They were kindred spirits in many ways and the instruction and thoughts Stephenson provided to Donovan about strategic and operational intelligence gathering, analysis, and operations would later provide Donovan with a strong basis for the creation of the COI / OSS.

On the European continent, Great Britain faced other issues from the quick collapse of France and the rest of Europe to the Germans. They were the only viable European military intact enough to deal with the Germans, however without a land base on the continent Churchill and the British senior officers were reluctant to do anything more than small-scale raids along the French coastline. Also, German and Italian progress in the Mediterranean region gave concern as to the security of several British garrisons throughout the Mediterranean Sea enroute to the Suez Canal. These concerns led to looking at alternative actions against the Axis.

One of these actions was a desperate action against the remaining French fleet. After the collapse of France, Churchill, his senior government and military leaders were desperate to gain control of this fleet. On July 3, 1940, the British Navy launched a series of attacks on the French fleet in an attempt to destroy or severely damage the vessels.

> The British Navy therefore boarded and took over French warships in British ports and in Egypt, with only token resistance. But at Mers el-Kebir, the port of Oran in western Algeria, the French commanding admiral, Marcel-Bruno Gensoul, refused after several hours' parley to accept the British ultimatum to proceed to some British or neutral port, safe from the Germans. Acting under irrevocable orders from Churchill's war cabinet, the British Mediterranean Fleet thereupon destroyed or crippled many French warships, killing or wounding about two thousand French sailors.[3]

The outcome was that the British Navy did not destroy the French fleet completely. The French nation and the French Navy in particular, was highly incensed against the British after this action. As a result of the attack, Vichy France forced Prime Minister Churchill to break all remaining diplomatic ties and to remove all British government officials from France and all of its remaining territory.

According to Robert Murphy, who had just taken over as the Chargé d'affaires to the Vichy government for the United States, "The effect on the French naval officers in North Africa was catastrophic and caused us endless difficulties there later."[4] When Britain broke diplomatic ties with Vichy France after the attempted destruction of the fleet, the structured British intelligence apparatus had to depart France and its colonies. To replace the lost collection capability, in July 1941, Britain established a Polish led clandestine intelligence operation under the control of Major M.Z. "Rygor" Slowikoski in French North Africa.

The British focused much of their intelligence collection efforts on the Mediterranean Sea area to secure their shipments to the beleaguered Eighth Army in Egypt, and to the remaining garrisons on various islands in the area. Any action in French North Africa created an opportunity to continue to fight the Germans and reduce the threat to the remaining garrisons. This drove Prime Minister Churchill to urge President Roosevelt to action in French North Africa, long before America was ready to commit forces anywhere.

<u>France</u>

On June 22, 1940, France capitulated to Nazi Germany and signed the armistice terms with Adolf Hitler who allowed the creation of a new French government at Vichy, the famous spa in the Auvergne region of France. Marshal Henri-Philippe Pétain, the French World War I hero of the battle of Verdun had become the French Head of State six days earlier. He sued for peace with Hitler in order to prevent a greater death toll, which France could ill-afford after its tremendous losses of soldiers in World War I. After the French Armistice went into effect on June 25, 1940, the German divisions gradually pulled back from the Spanish frontier and approximately one-third of continental France. This formally established the split between the occupied and unoccupied regions of France.

The remaining senior French civil and military leadership split into two groups Free France and Vichy France by the end of the summer in 1940. General de Gaulle, who maintained diplomatic connections with Great Britain, led Free France based in England. However, he was not well known or liked by his fellow French officers and civilian leaders outside of England. These men could not understand why he would go against Marshal Pétain and continued to disregard him and put down any support for the Free French in the unoccupied territories and the colonies. President Roosevelt also did not trust him initially. In agreement with Prime Minister Churchill, Roosevelt told the military planners for Operation TORCH to keep their plans a secret from de Gaulle until the invasion of French North Africa started. The Vichy Government under Marshal Pétain maintained diplomatic relations with the United States, but remained a semi-independent puppet state of Hitler's. The Pétain led government still held overall control of the French colonies, but had decentralized much of the legal authority to the colonial governors, granting them a level of self-autonomy. The Americans and British hoped, in late 1941, that any invasion of France or its colonies, specifically French Morocco and Algeria, would release the French from the negotiated armistice with Germany and provide Vichy France a way to enter the war on the Allied side. This would also allow the Allies to support the resistance in France and in North Africa against the Germans, with complete cooperation of the government. Yet, in French North Africa,

> The only invaders [of North Africa] then envisaged were the British. After the capitulation of France, French sentiment had turned sharply against their former ally. Many Frenchmen blamed their defeat on British reluctance to bring more airplanes to the continent during the campaign. They resented British withdrawal to their home islands and their refusal to surrender. The French were also embittered by the attacks of British warships against the French fleet to keep the vessels from falling into German hands. They were incensed by British support

of General Charles de Gaulle who, from London, sought to continue the struggle against the Axis.[5]

Internally the French people were at loss as to what to do. Many thought the old Marshal was correct in capitulating in order to survive and then thrive under German control until they were strong enough to throw off the Germans. This thought was especially strong in the officer corps. Others wanted to counterattack against the Germans, but they knew the French military, such as it was, was not capable. The majority of officers in French North Africa desired to defend what was left of the empire and wait until the time was right to regain control of France proper. They could not rely on their oldest ally since 1852, the British, because they supported de Gaulle, whom no one understood, and had attacked their fleet without provocation. The French could only look towards their other historical ally the United States, who was neutral until December 1941.

To put some of the personalities and their political and loyalty leanings in place, the following is a list of the key leaders in French North Africa and their perceived support to the Allies, Vichy France, and or to the Axis.

> *Admiral Jean Francois Darlan*: Commander-in-Chief French Armed Forces (in North Africa more or less by accident), Anglophobe, and committed to the Axis (and hence mistrusted by the Allies). However, he was now thought to be wavering, and, if faced with an Allied *fait accompli*, might throw his weight on the winning side. His position assured him the loyalty of the majority of French military leaders and therefore made his attitude all-important to the success of an Allied invasion.

> *General Alphonse Juin*: Commander-in-Chief French military forces in North Africa. Anti-Axis. Had prepared undercover plans for resisting any Axis invasion of French North Africa but was unwilling to defy Vichy. Could be labeled as cautiously pro-Allies.

> *General Auguste Paul Nogués*: Resident General of Morocco, at Rabat. Had the reputation of being pro-Vichy, which had earned him the hostility of the anti-Vichy French. Very influential among the natives in Morocco, and for that reason

more useful to the Americans in office than if removed (as many demanded). Not to be counted as pro-Allies.

M. Yves Châtel: Governor General of Algeria. One of the few civilians in a high administrative post. Pro-Vichy.

Major General Charles Mast: Commanding Officer, Algerian Division. Pro-Allies and in touch with Robert D. Murphy and General Henri Giraud.

Major General Emile Béthouart: Commanding Officer, Casablanca Division. (Pro-Allies and in touch with Robert D. Murphy).[6]

With the exception of Béthouart, all these men took their orders from Pétain via Darlan and down their respective chains of command. They were not about to welcome the Americans or any other invader warmly, but were willing to co-operate with the Americans based on orders from above. The French question, based on its senior leaders would remain the key question throughout the planning and execution of the operation. Allied intelligence and diplomatic efforts were concentrated on understanding what that answer would be and based on the above list of just seven senior leaders, it was not easy to understand. Even in the last few hours before the invasion, the unexpected presence of Darlan in Algiers caused Murphy to alter some of the plans. Darlan was the key not only to the invasion and French defense against it, but also to the remaining French fleet.

Because of the complications with the senior leaders in French North Africa, Allied strategic and operational intelligence collection was difficult in the region. The internal strife among these leaders and Vichy made the Axis' control of the region simple, but for the Allies it was a diplomatic and intelligence mess. The purpose of this paper is not to focus on the political and diplomatic issues, but to examine the advance force operation requirements as discussed and only incorporating these personality and politically charged issues as they pertained to the collection of information for the planning and execution of Operation TORCH.

United States

When World War II began, the United States declared itself neutral. Isolationists pushed heavily to keep "America's boys from fighting Europe's War". President Roosevelt was facing one of the most difficult times of his political career; he was running for the Presidency for a previously unheard of third consecutive time. Yet, Roosevelt looked toward the Japanese actions in the Pacific and the German actions in Europe and knew instinctively that the United States would be involved sooner rather than later on both fronts. Publicly he supported the neutral stance called for by the isolationists and the majority of Americans to ensure his winning of the 1940 election, but privately Roosevelt began to posture the United States for a potential role in both regions.

After he became President of the United States, Roosevelt personally worked on many projects to reinvigorate the military for combat operations across all echelons, to include modernizing the United States intelligence organizations. He knew that most of the intelligence apparatus was still stuck with techniques used in the Spanish-American War of 1898-1902.

> In 1939 President Roosevelt took over personally, as Commander in Chief, the supervision of the somewhat desultory deliberations of the Joint Army-Navy Board, which had existed for many years to insure 'cooperation and coordination' of all 'joint action of the Army and Navy relative to national defense.' …It was, nevertheless, in 1941 the only rudimentary high command the nation had, and it decided to make a stab, at least in principle, at providing an intelligence base to underpin its deliberations. General Marshall, Chief of Staff of the Army, and the capable Chief of Naval Operations, Admiral Harold R. (Betty) Stark, ordered the establishment of a Joint Intelligence Committee (JIC) as a central information

group serving the Joint Board. The order was approved on October 1, 1941, setting up the Joint Army Navy Intelligence Committee.[7]

This landmark decision attempted to create a centralized strategic level military intelligence organization whose purpose was to analyze potential international threats to the nation. Prior to this order, the United States had only small cells in the Army's Military Intelligence Division (MID) and the Office of Naval Intelligence (ONI). These intelligence organizations were supposed to provide the needed intelligence base for military and or civil actions outside of the United States and its territories. However, as with most departments of the United States military in the interwar period, they were understaffed and underfunded. Most of the intelligence provided to government senior leaders came through Naval attachés, who were serving in seventeen posts, nine in Europe and eight in South America. Eighty people comprised the Army's Military Intelligence Division, or G-2. The division was largely a housekeeping service, running loyalty checks on War Department personnel, protecting government buildings, bridges, and other facilities, and conducting meager intelligence.[8] Other government agencies such as the Department's of State and Justice had equally limited staffing and levels of effort to first gather and then analyze the intelligence information received was just as limited in providing a comprehensive report on any other country and their actions.

In order to make some sense of the intelligence chaos he inherited, on June 26, 1939, President Roosevelt ordered the heads of the FBI, MID, and ONI to start synchronizing their actions. He handed responsibility for this thankless task to the assistant secretary of state for administration, George S. Messersmith. At this stage, President Roosevelt had no thought of creating a central intelligence service. He was not ready, nor was the country.[9] However, within two short years, President Roosevelt was ready and saw a need for a revolutionary new concept in peacetime - a civilian, central coordinating intelligence system. He established the short-lived Office of the Coordinator of Information (COI), in July 1941, and subsequently in 1942 rechristened it with the better-known name, the Office of Strategic Services (OSS). President Roosevelt did this to frustrate FBI Director J. Edgar Hoover's ambitions of controlling information at the senior levels and in order to have an independent organization conduct the tasks of intelligence collection and analysis he foresaw would become desperately needed in the coming war.[10]

Through the influences of the British senior military and political leadership, the United States Secretary of the Navy William Franklin "Frank" Knox, and the boldness and foresight of Colonel William J. "Wild Bill" Donovan, the necessity and reason for a centralized intelligence organization where quickly realized. President Roosevelt gave Donovan a Presidential Directive establishing COI officially on July 11, 1941. This became the first established civilian intelligence organization within the United States charged with collecting, analyzing, and providing intelligence to the President of the United States and senior members of the government. COI also provided the structure Prime Minister Churchill envisioned for the passing of intelligence information to the United States without compromising the source of the information.

Advance Force Operations

President Roosevelt authorized the founding of COI/OSS to conduct strategic intelligence collection, analysis and advance force operations for the United States, under civilian leadership. These intelligence collection and analysis activities and advance force operations at the strategic levels gather intelligence information, develop

relationships with foreign officials and leaders, understand the operational and

intelligence environment of a country and or region, and as necessary help to establish or

reinforce existing resistance forces. However, COI/OSS also found itself conducting

these needed requirements at the operational level, leading to a blurring of the levels of

information requirements and the authority levels needed to authorize specific advance

force operations, such as the removal of indigenous people from the region for

operational needs.

Operationally, United States Joint Doctrine states, "Advance force operations

range from reconnaissance to bombardment of the landing area by air, naval surface fires,

and even artillery if firing positions are available. Overt actions are usually meant to

either shape the battlespace within the operational area or to deceive the adversary as to

the real objectives."[11] There are multiple tasks required of an advance force. The tasks

on which this paper will analyze the OSS' abilities are:

> Supporting, Advance Force, and Pre-assault Operations
> (4) Hydrographic reconnaissance, obstacle clearance, and preparation of the
> landing beaches and seaward approaches;
> (5) Reconnaissance and surveillance of A[dvance] F[orce] objectives, landing
> beaches, L[anding] Z[one]s, D[rop] Z[one]s, and high speed avenues of approach
> into the landing area. The collection effort should focus on satisfying priority
> intelligence requirements (PIRs) and determining if the required conditions for the
> assault have been established.
> (6) Neutralization or destruction of adversary high-payoff targets.[12]

The President of the United States directed both Murphy and Donovan to conduct

strategic and operational advance force operations. Each of their elements supported

most if not all of the current doctrinal requirements of advance force operations.

The United States remained, at the onset of hostilities in the Europe and North Africa, greatly hampered by the lack of capability in its existing intelligence agencies. Without the foresight of the President of the United States, the Prime Minister of Great Britain, and others like Colonel William J. Donovan and Mr. Robert Murphy, the United States would have been in a far worse intelligence posture in the summer of 1942 as it prepared for combat operations in French North Africa and against General Rommel's Afrika Korps. This paper will contend that because of the Allied intelligence agencies successful conduct of strategic and operational advance force operations in French North Africa in 1940-1942, the planners and executors of Operation TORCH ultimately received the required intelligence requested for effective planning and execution of Operation TORCH.

---

[1] Patrick K. O'Donnell. *Operatives, Spies, and Saboteurs: The Unknown Story of the Men and Women of World War II's OSS*. New York: Free Press, 2004. xi.

[2] Robert D. Murphy. *Diplomat Among Warriors*. Garden City, N.Y.: Doubleday, 1964. 79.

[3] Ibid. 53.

[4] Ibid. 55.

[5] Martin Blumenson. *Mark Clark*. New York: Congdon & Weed, 1984. 66.

[6] Jack Coggins. *The Campaign for North Africa*. Garden City, N.Y.: Doubleday, 1980. 60.

[7] Ray S Cline. *Secrets, Spies, and Scholars Blueprint of the Essential CIA*. Washington: Acropolis Books, 1976. 18.

[8] Joseph E.Perisco. *Roosevelt's Secret War*. New York: Random House, 2001. 96.

[9] Ibid. 17.

[10] Cline, *Secrets, Spies, and Scholars Blueprint of the Essential CIA*, 21.

[11] U.S. Department of Defense. Joint Publication 3-02.1 Joint Tactics, Techniques, and Procedures for Landing Force Operations. Washington, DC: Government Printing Office, 2004. IV-3.

[12] Ibid. IV-3.

CHAPTER 2

AMERICAN DIPLOMATIC INTELLIGENCE

> For the first time in this era Americans listed as diplomatic officials found themselves competing for scraps of information in the cafes and casinos with foreign diplomats and assorted spies of all countries. Within a few weeks these 'vice-consuls' were sending descriptive reporting to Washington responsive to the requirements for information left with Donovan and Roosevelt by [Commander] Ian Fleming [of the British Naval Intelligence] during his visit to Washington in June 1941.
>
> -Ray S. Cline, *Secrets, Spies, and Scholars Blueprint of the Essential CIA*[1]

In early June 1940, the United States ambassador and staff still resided in the United States Embassy in Paris, France. By the end of the month, most of the staff departed for the United States and the remaining officers moved to Vichy, France, to remain with Marshal Pétain and his government. Two of the senior members of the United States Embassy who departed Paris for Vichy were Robert D. Murphy, the Charges d'affaires and the naval attaché Commander Roscoe H. Hillenkoetter. These two men and their information on Vichy France would help to develop and later drive President Roosevelt's first military plan for American involvement against Nazi Germany.

During the summer of 1940, the Nazi occupation of France settled into the areas just outside of the unoccupied territories and away from the Spanish border, the United States Embassy staff continued to develop their diplomatic contacts and level of trust with the leaders of the Vichy government. The diplomat's effectiveness throughout this tumultuous time developed the diplomatic and operational conditions needed to invade French North Africa and created a second front against General Rommel in Libya.

Commander Hillenkoetter, a Naval Academy graduate who would eventually command the USS *Missouri,* and become the first director of the Central Intelligence Agency from May 1, 1947 to October 7, 1950, journeyed to French North Africa in late June and early July 1940. This trip occurred during the transition between the Third Republic's collapse and the completion of the move to Vichy. He went to assess the conditions of both the French military and government in French Morocco and Algeria. Commander Hillenkoetter returned to Vichy to submit, in combination with Mr. Murphy's assessment of the political and diplomatic affairs in Vichy, this first report on the status of French North Africa back to the Department of State in Washington in August 1940.

> Hillenkoetter was agreeably surprised and encouraged by what he observed during his brief excursion. Contrary to rumors, which were being broadcast from London, he found that the Nazis had left French Africa almost completely to its own devices. He said only a few German consuls and Italian members of the Armistice Commission were in evidence, while Frenchmen were administering the territories practically the same as before the war. Furthermore, said our naval attaché, the military establishment was far stronger than he had expected, with about 125,000 combat-trained men on active service and about 200,000 more in reserve. Hillenkoetter added that these experienced army, navy and air force officers and men had not lost their traditional French fighting spirit. They had accepted the German armistice and had sworn allegiance to the Pétain Government, but they were confident they could protect and control their African empire despite the collapse of the mother country. 'The atmosphere over there is not comparable to the confusion in Vichy,' Hillenkoetter told us. 'If France is going to fight again anywhere in this war, I believe North Africa will be the place.' He impressed us all with his hopefulness, which was reflected in the reports our Vichy Embassy sent to Washington.[2]

Unknown to Murphy and Hillenkoetter, President Roosevelt took a special interest in this report and further reports made about the Vichy government by Murphy. These accounts would help to formulate his plan for supporting the French, while preparing to attack the Germans, when the time was right.

President Roosevelt further turned to Robert Murphy to use his connections, analysis, and information gathering skills in Vichy France. Robert Daniel Murphy was an Irish-American Catholic born in Milwaukee in 1894. He held a Bachelor of Laws from Marquette University, a Jesuit school in Milwaukee, and obtained his master's degree at George Washington University. Murphy had joined the United States Post Office as a clerk, then, transferred to the Consular Service, serving at Bern, Zurich, Munich, Seville, and lastly in Paris for the past ten years. "Thus it came about that I [Murphy] was officially in charge of our embassy on July 3, 1940 - one of the most unfortunate dates in the long history of Anglo-French relations."[3] It was the attack on the French naval fleet by the British Navy, which severely hampered any further direct British actions in French North Africa and seriously upset support of the Allies, but the British in particular, by French officers and governments during the early part of the Second World War. Robert Murphy was now the lead American diplomat in Vichy charged to understand all of the intricacies of this new government and report them back to Washington.

In mid-September 1940, President Roosevelt requested Mr. Murphy return to Washington D.C. for a meeting. The Under Secretary of State, Sumner Welles told Murphy that the President had read the reports on French North Africa carefully and now President Roosevelt summoned Murphy to see him.[4] President Roosevelt was intrigued at the possibilities for some level of action in French North Africa, because of its unique status under the French-German armistice. It remained semi-independent from Vichy France control with limited oversight by a joint German-Italian Armistice Committee, whose job was to oversee the movement of goods such as rubber latex, grain, and oil into

Italy and Germany for the Axis war effort and report on any suspicious anti-Axis activity. President Roosevelt believed North Africa would be a very likely place for French troops to return to the war against Nazi Germany based on the reports from Murphy, Hillenkoetter, and others he had tasked with gathering information in the region.

When Murphy arrived at the White House, he went into the President's office, where in front of the President was a large map showing all of French North and West Africa. President Roosevelt told Murphy that he had given much thought about how to help French officers in French North Africa. Murphy provided some of the insights he had gathered from Hillenkoetter and others in Vichy. President Roosevelt also tasked Murphy, during their meeting, to connect with General Maxime Weygand, Vichy France's Governor of North Africa and ascertain "his real authority in the region, what did the old soldier have in mind for the future, and what could the United States do to encourage him?"[5] After further discussions, the President concluded the meeting by telling Murphy to return to Vichy and work subtly to get permission to make a thorough inspection tour of French Africa and to report his findings back to the President. The President's personal policy thus became the United States Government French African policy. President Roosevelt also told Murphy, "If you learn anything in Africa of special interest, send it to me. Don't bother going through State Department channels." [6] Mr. Murphy had just become another of President Roosevelt's "personal representatives," like "Wild Bill" Donovan.

Murphy departed the White House and started to research French North Africa in the secret files of various United States government departments. He discovered that most of the departments in the government had no real interest in Africa and that military and naval attachés had given it cursory attention. Because of this lack of information

resident from the United States, Murphy looked at documents assembled in France,

Britain, Italy, and Germany, many of which were not translated into English.[7] Armed

with what little additional information he could gather from the archives, Murphy

departed Washington for Vichy, France. Working through diplomatic channels, he

gained permission from the Vichy government to enter French North Africa.

A few weeks later, on December 18, 1940, Mr. Murphy departed France for

Algiers and began his three-week fact-finding mission throughout French North Africa.

When he arrived in Algiers, he received word that General Weygand was in Dakar and

immediately departed to meet with him there. General Weygand and his associates

were forthcoming with information to Murphy, not only the material facts, but also

confiding in their sentiments and intentions. These sentiments and intentions were full of

the rumors of a German invasion and the implications of such actions. This led Weygand

to look for some kind of support from the United States as a way of countering that

rumor. This led to the first discussion about the possibilities of some type of economic

agreement between the United States and French North African colonies. Mr. Murphy

concluded his trip after having seen each of the major cities in the region and gathering

his facts and information for the President. He departed for Lisbon, Portugal on January

5, 1941, enroute back to Washington.

The Murphy-Weygand Accord

Upon returning to Washington, Murphy filed his reports, which were so well

received by the President that he sent Murphy back to North Africa in February 1941 to

negotiate an economic agreement with General Weygand and the Vichy government.

23

Under the conditions of the agreement, the United States would continue to trade with the French colonies as long as the United States was able to post additional food control officers in Algeria, Morocco, and Tunisia to observe the shipments and see that they did not go to Nazi Germany. These food control officers would become vice-consuls working under Murphy, whose true intent was to act as clandestine intelligence officers to collect secret information on North Africa and France itself. [8] Since the job of these vice-consuls was to supervise the shipments, all involved including Pétain and Weygand understood that these men would really be intelligence agents, therefore not working totally in a clandestine role.

> A few farsighted men in Washington had become aware of how little we knew about what was going on in Africa. They saw the need for dependable American observers, instead of having to rely entirely upon our French colleagues. We had American consulates in five French African cities, staffed by about a dozen officers altogether, but these State Department officials had been trained only for duties normally associated with their work. It was decided, therefore, that we now must appoint a dozen observers, whom we would call vice consuls, and that this special group would work under my personal direction. [9]

General Weygand understood that these were unusual times in diplomacy and made several other unusual concessions regarding the safeguarding of classified information, use of lock bags without inspection and the use of secret codes for normal diplomatic use. This concession extended to all of the consular staffs, including the twelve new "vice consuls". [10] This intelligence opportunity was without precedent. The United States was given carte blanche opportunity to spy on not only the French, but also the Germans and the Italians working in French North Africa and more importantly safely move their information out to the senior government and military leadership in Washington without interruption and interception by the French and therefore by the German-Italian

Commissions as well. Robert Murphy had also successfully secured the support and understanding of the Vichy government through this economic agreement and by doing so, implied to France that the United States would not abandon them. It also sent a signal to the French that American was willing to continue to work together, as long as the goods and services remained out of Axis hands.

Because of his success with the accords, in the spring of 1941, the State Department officially assigned Murphy as United States Consul to Algeria. His responsibilities also included running an undercover intelligence gathering operation in Algiers and at outposts for the twelve vice-consuls, who were authorized under the designation "food control officers."

The Vice Consuls

Part of the secret rationale for Washington's agreement with the economic accord and the broader policy with Vichy was the intelligence value of a diplomatic presence in France. By the spring of 1941, members of the French army's intelligence service who were anti-German, secretly transmitted military and political information to the American military attaché at Vichy, Colonel Robert Schow. It was now vitally important to have intelligence personnel in French North Africa to perform intelligence duties. Cordell Hull, the Secretary of State agreed with the War Department on this point and stated that his 'food control officers' should perform these duties.

The task for selecting the staff went to Assistant Secretary of State Adolf Berle. He admitted, "at once that our limited number of regular Foreign Service vice consuls could not provide the specialized personnel called for by this project, involving as it did a certain amount of irregular activity and danger."[11] Berle found the answer to the

25

manning question in a commodity the State Department did not have, experienced Army and Navy officers, who could appreciate objects and events of military significance.

The State Department persuaded the chiefs of the Army and Navy intelligence to support their idea for filling vice-consul positions with Army and Navy officers. However, the Services did not have an officer qualified in Arabic and had always relied on the British and French services for information about the Mediterranean and North Africa areas. They placed these twelve men under the guiding hand of Wallace Phillips, an expatriate businessman who headed the American Chamber of Commerce in London (who later became Donovan's first espionage advisor). They learned French culture and politics in order to serve as North African "Vice Consuls" under Murphy's direction.

Issues in time and delays by the War Department were abundant. One of the primary issues arose from the fact that a military officer could not directly work for the Department of State, undercover or otherwise. This was due to the different budgets between the individual departments, the War Department, the Department of the Navy, and the Department of State and the question of who paid the salary for the officers. Most importantly to the officers selected was the question of their legal status as military officers under the Geneva Convention regarding spies in case of capture. Under the Geneva Convention, if they were captured spying the punishment could be death. The Joint Chiefs of Staff decision was that the twelve volunteers would "resign" their commissions and work directly for the Department of State under Robert Murphy, yet be guided by Wallace Phillips, in London, and organized as members of the "K Organization" belonging to the Office of Naval Intelligence.

The men selected were reservists selected from all occupations, which helped to relieve some of the stress of the legalities because they could be "hired" by the Department of State as full-time employees legally, not in military status. Collectively they were nicknamed the "twelve disciples" or "twelve apostles". Murphy was to be their boss, yet they would work out of each of the consulates in French Morocco and Algeria for the resident consuls. The resident consuls would not know of their true function until long after the invasion. Thirteen men were selected, only twelve made it through the entire time. The men selected were:

> Stafford Reid, a construction man from New York; Sidney Bartlett, a California oil man; Leland Rounds, a businessman; John Knox, who had graduated from the French Military Academy at St. Cyr; John Boyd, who had been a Coca-Cola branch manager in Marseilles; Harry Woodruff and John Utter, two bankers who had lived in Paris; Franklin Canfield, a young lawyer; Donald Coster, an advertising man[who was later sent home for improprieties]; Kenneth Pendar, a Harvard librarian who was later to write a book based on his adventures; Carleton Coon, a Harvard anthropologist; Ridgeway Knight, a wine merchant; and Gordon Browne, who had previously traveled in Morocco. [12]

Time and government red tape were at odds with the necessity of these men arriving quickly to start the supervision of the shipments. However, the shipments to French North Africa as a part of the accords had not started as promised either. The first group of vice-consuls arrived in Algiers on June 10, 1941, with the remainder arriving in July. They began their work immediately, acquiring maps, charting fields, measuring coastlines, sounding out French and Arab sentiment, watching ship movements, and trying to make up plausible stories for their superiors, the United States consuls, which would explain their so frequent absence from their offices. [13] Even though the twelve men had little to no training in espionage, they all volunteered, and because of their varied livelihoods in the United States, they were able to adapt quickly to their respective environments and provide the information required.

The vice consuls were stationed under consular cover throughout the region at Casablanca, Safi, Oran, Algiers, Bizerte, and Tunis. They gathered intelligence on the German and Italian armistice commissions, reported the movements of the French fleet, and make contact with anti-Vichy elements both French colonialists and the indigenous groups. Their effectiveness in their tasks will be discussed in the following chapters, but the Gestapo and the German-Italian Armistice Commissions in the various cities showed that these vice consuls had successfully concealed their activities.

> The Gestapo paid little attention to the Vice Consuls. 'Since all their thoughts,' read a German report, "are centered on their social, sexual, or culinary interests, petty quarrels and jealousies are daily incidents with them. Altogether they represent a perfect picture of the mixture of races and characters in that savage conglomeration called the United States of America, and anyone who observes them can well judge the state of mind and instability that must be prevalent in their country today… Lack of pluck and democratic degeneracy prevails among them, resulting from their too easy life, corrupt morals, and consequent lack of energy…They are totally lacking in method, organization and discipline… We can only congratulate ourselves on the selection of this group of enemy agents who will give us no trouble.' But the Nazis had miscalculated. Within weeks, Murphy's amateur spies were flooding Washington with valuable reports on all significant military and political developments in the colonies. Six months later, when the Japanese attack plunged the United States into the war, this intelligence proved essential to America's strategic planning.[14]

The reported effectiveness of the vice-consuls was based on the intelligence collected and passed on to Washington D.C. before the United States was a formal belligerent in the war. According to the OSS archives, what these men accomplished in their support of advance force operations was incredible. These amateur American spies had gone out to provide operational level intelligence on all forces present in French North Africa and prepared the operational and intelligence battlefield, long before the President gave the final approval for military action. The question remains as to how effective were they before and after their merger with the OSS.

28

[1] Cline, *Secrets, Spies, and Scholars Blueprint of the Essential CIA*, 45.

[2] Murphy, *Diplomat Among Warriors*, 66-67.

[3] Ibid. 53.

[4] Ibid. 67.

[5] Ibid. 73.

[6] Ibid. 68.

[7] Ibid. 70.

[8] Cline, *Secrets, Spies, and Scholars Blueprint of the Essential CIA*, 44.

[9] Murphy, *Diplomat Among Warriors*, 89.

[10] R. Harris Smith. *OSS: the Secret History of America's First Central Intelligence Agency*. Berkeley: University of California Press, 1972. 38.

[11] Murphy, *Diplomat Among Warriors*, 88.

[12] Allen Welsh Dulles. *Great True Spy Stories*. New York: Harper & Row, 1968. 382.

[13] Ibid. 382.

[14] Smith, *OSS: the Secret History of America's First Central Intelligence Agency*, 39.

CHAPTER 3

THE ORIGINS OF COI / OSS

'For us, in the United States,' declared William J. Casey in 1974, 'it all began with a New York lawyer who saw his country facing a deadly menace and knew that it was unprepared and uninformed. It's hard for us to realize today that there was a time in 1940 and 1941 when William J. Donovan was a one-man CIA for President Roosevelt.'
- Thomas F. Troy *Wild Bill and Intrepid Donovan, Stephenson, and the Origin of CIA.*[1]

The State of United States Intelligence

As Europe went to war, the United States lacked the capability at the national level to work in back alleys and gin joints with thieves, pickpockets, safe crackers, and anyone else who was less than desirable. Unlike Great Britain, which had established its spy service publically in 1909, Germany in 1913, Russia in 1917, and France in 1935, the United States did not have a centralized intelligence gathering organization until the summer of 1941. What the United States had was a loose conglomeration of organizations within the government that was organized to conduct intelligence collection and analysis, but only in gentlemen-like actions. Each of these organizations, such as the signals intelligence and codebreaking group were underfunded and undermanned. These organizations competed for whatever funding they could as well as jockeying for position among the key political leaders in the government. This would all change within the course of two years. By the summer of 1941, the United States government was hiring people who could do all of those dirty, nasty espionage tasks; stealing state secrets from embassies, seducing other country's agents, parachuting in behind enemy lines to create resistance groups, and of course, gathering information for commanders to use in their planning and execution of a war.

However, in the interwar period, there was an intelligence vacuum. The public outcry after the attack on Pearl Harbor on December 7, 1941, only highlighted the true state of intelligence collection and analysis in the United States. President Roosevelt and key members of his government had known this fact for much longer. Joseph Perisco states in his book, *Roosevelt's Secret War,* that after taking office and evaluating the intelligence provided by the FBI, the Army's G-2 and the Navy's Office of Naval Intelligence, the President felt

> Undeniably, an intelligence vacuum had to be filled. Even before the war, FDR had expressed his exasperation to his secretary of state Cordell Hull. The Federal Bureau of Investigation, the Army's Military Intelligence Division, and the Office of Naval Intelligence were 'constantly crossing each other's tracks,' he complained to Hull. This duplication was wasteful, expensive, and inefficient, the President charged. He wanted the activities of the three agencies sensibly coordinated.[2]

In true Roosevelt fashion, he stated this need openly, but he also attempted to fill the vacuum personally. President Roosevelt recruited friends, such as millionaire William Vincent Astor, who worked directly for Roosevelt collecting intelligence information in New York, and started directing government employees such as J. Edgar Hoover, the Director of the FBI, and Secretary of State Cordell Hull to fill in the known intelligence gaps across the globe. It was through Hull that the President first tasked George S. Messersmith, the Assistant Secretary of State for Administration, to perform the role of synchronizing intelligence information gathered across the world, which came into the four government offices of the MID, ONI, FBI, and Department of State. Even with this initial set up, President Roosevelt still called on individuals to work directly for him to gather information on problem areas of the world. One of these individuals was Colonel

William Joseph Donovan.

Colonel William J. Donovan

Donovan was a World War I Medal of Honor recipient, a Hoover Republican, an Irish Catholic, and a millionaire Wall Street lawyer who had a deep desire to ensure his country was armed with the information necessary to defeat its potential enemies. He was also a free thinker who remembered much of the fifth column activity of World War I and was determined that such influences should not come to America in this war. However, the government could use these fifth column activities against the Nazis' and Japanese, if the opportunity presented itself.

President Roosevelt first called upon Donovan when FDR was the Assistant Secretary of the Navy, to go to on fact-finding trips. Donovan first travelled to Siberia in 1920 to observe and report on anti-Bolshevik operations and Japanese activities. Later in 1935-36, Donovan went to Ethiopia to observe the Italian Army and its actions. Donovan departed for Ethiopia, but first stopped in Italy and received directly from Benito Mussolini, the Prime Minister of Italy, his personal permission to travel to Ethiopia with the condition that he return to Italy and provide an unbiased report on the Italian actions in which Donovan was to observe in the Horn of Africa region. After two months of travel, Donovan returned to Washington via Rome where he reported to President Roosevelt on his observations and analysis of the Italian Army actions in Ethiopia and his time spent with Mussolini. Next FDR sent Donovan to Spain to report on the ongoing Spanish Civil War. Again, on July 16, 1940, President Roosevelt sent Donovan on another fact-finding mission, this time to England to provide a second look at the British defenses, their will to survive the air raids, and their will to fight, as German Luftwaffe executed the first phases of Operation Sea Lion, the planned invasion of the British Isles. Donovan returned from England and reported to the President that Great Britain would hold on physically and that Prime Minister Churchill was strengthening the will of the people to stand firm through their darkest hour.

Donovan's assessment was contrary to the then United States Ambassador to Great Britain, Joseph Kennedy, who fretted that the British would lose faith and heart in the struggle and ultimately capitulate, as had France. Kennedy stated to President Roosevelt that Great Britain would not be able to withstand the onslaught of the German Luftwaffe without aid from America. Because of Kennedy's attitude, gloom analysis and other indiscretions, FDR would later recall the ambassador, but in Donovan, he continued to find an unbiased and non-partisan appraiser of the events he saw and someone who could correctly analyze and synthesize this information into relevant intelligence for the President and Senior Government leaders.

Donovan's trips made him, as William Casey declared, "a one-man CIA for President Roosevelt."[3] Donovan not only became President Roosevelt's single man intelligence agency, when called upon, but he personally executed official strategic level intelligence gathering on multiple occasions in areas where future operations might be possible. Because President Roosevelt was detail and information hungry, he provided clear guidance to Colonel Donovan on the specific information and intelligence he wanted as Donovan traveled in the regions. These specified information and intelligence requirements are much the same as those required in today's advance force operations at strategic levels.

In November 1940, President Roosevelt again used Donovan's ability for appraising events in the world, this time to the Mediterranean area. He requested

Donovan to undertake a mission to make a strategic appreciation of the Mediterranean

region from an economic, political and military standpoint. Donovan accepted without

hesitation. Donovan saw this as an opportunity to see for himself the importance of the

Mediterranean region in the upcoming war. In August 1940, he had stressed particularly

the necessity of some kind of agreement with the French in order to secure American

interests in Northwest Africa to President Roosevelt.[4] This trip also included multiple

introductions of Donovan to the British Intelligence apparatus in its entirety, and included

a personal meeting with Prime Minister Churchill. William "Intrepid" Stephenson

arranged the London itinerary with the intent of introducing Donovan to the entirety of

the British Intelligence apparatus for a full appreciation of its capabilities. Stephenson

also intended these introductions to the British Intelligence organization and its

capabilities to inspire Donovan with further thoughts on establishing a like arrangement

for the United States. Donovan was very eager for this part of the trip, as was President

Roosevelt.

Donovan departed with Stephenson on December 6, 1940, for London. He

traveled for three and a half months throughout the Mediterranean area after completing

his introductions in London, visiting Gibraltar, Malta, Egypt, Greece, Bulgaria,

Yugoslavia, and Portugal. He returned to the United States on March 18, 1941 and on

the following day, accompanied by Secretary of the Navy Frank Knox, he made the first

of a series of calls at the White House to report to the President. During these meetings,

Donovan stressed three points: first, the gravity of the shipping problem in and around

the Mediterranean Sea due to Italian and German naval activity; second, the dangers and the opportunities which the situation in French Northwest Africa represented for the United States; and third, the extraordinary importance of psychological and political elements in the war and the necessity of making the most of these elements in planning and executing national policies.[5] Donovan's points and supporting assessments provided President Roosevelt with a clear understanding of the events and activities the Axis were conducting and the implications of them in the Mediterranean area outside of those provided by Robert Murphy and his staff in Vichy. It is also now evident that President Roosevelt had enough information presented to him from his own reliable sources to make his own decision on whether or not to attack North Africa as America's first objective in the war. Many historians have written about Prime Minister Churchill's influence on President Roosevelt's decision to plan for and conduct Operation TORCH. However, the argument can be made that President Roosevelt had already decided to make French North Africa a primary focus for the United States prior to the first wartime conference in December 1941 based on the reports from Murphy and Hillenkoetter in mid to late 1940, as well as Donovan and Murphy's independent travels in late 1940 and early 1941.

The Office of the Coordinator of Information (COI)

Donovan was one of the few Americans around the President with recent experience abroad and with a good understanding of the events, key persons involved, and scope of the impacts made by Nazi Germany and its allies across the world. He was also a strong candidate by virtue of his understanding for the need of a strong, centralized intelligence agency and because of his natural ability to create organizations, especially one that would be able to answer these intelligence requirements. This made him the ideal candidate to understand the intelligence requirements of the President and senior government leaders in a war against the Axis.

Upon his return from the Mediterranean region, Donovan held several meetings with the President. During these meetings, Donovan took the opportunity to present his ideas on creating a single civilian intelligence apparatus similar in scope and capability to both the British Special Operations Executive (SOE) and Secret Intelligence Service (SIS) the future MI-6. The President took the ideas in stride, but in typical Rooseveltian fashion, he left Donovan awaiting a decision for some time. President Roosevelt did think long and hard about the idea of creating an independent, civilian controlled agency capable of fulfilling the intelligence gathering and analysis gap that Donovan's concepts would fill. President Roosevelt made his decision final by using a "Military Order" dated June 25, 1941. This draft established the "position of Coordinator of Defense Intelligence" to operate "under the direction and supervision of the President" and designated Donovan as "Coordinator of Strategic Information."

> The key clause in this document granted Donovan the authority to collect and analyze information and data, military or otherwise, which may bear upon national defense strategy; to interpret and correlate such strategic information and data, and to make it available to the President and to such other officials as the President may determine, and to carry out, when requested by the President, such supplementary activities as may facilitate the security of strategic information not now available to the government.[6]

While this document establishing the Coordinator of Defense Intelligence seemed to have no official standing this Military Order helped to create the official July 11, 1941, Presidential Directive, which established the Office of Coordinator of Information (COI). The Office of Coordinator of Information was announced to the public as an agency for the collection and analysis of information and data organized officially under the executive office of the President of the United States, working directly for and funded by the President. In reality, COI and its successor, the Office of Strategic Services (OSS), began an organized venture into the fields of espionage, propaganda, subversion and related activities under the aegis of a centralized intelligence agency, a first for the United States.[7]

President Roosevelt formally named Colonel Donovan as the COI on the same day as he established the organization. Donovan, a Republican and a former political opponent in the gubernatorial race for New York in 1927, was not necessarily the man people would have expected Roosevelt to choose. "Yet Roosevelt had chosen him to direct the New Deal's excursion into espionage, sabotage, 'black' propaganda, guerilla warfare, and other 'un-American' subversive practices."[8] Donovan was elated with the position, but more importantly with the work, he was now officially hired to do.

Donovan set about quickly to establish the COI, specifically the Research and Analysis Branch first, using talent across academia to first analyze information on Germany, Italy, and French North Africa, presumably the same information Mr. Murphy had looked at nearly a year before and then to begin planning operations. Donovan set forth in his "Memorandum of Establishment of Service of Strategic Information" the relation of information to strategic planning in total warfare. He pointed out the inadequacy of the intelligence set-up then existing and stated:

> It is essential that we set up a central enemy intelligence organization which would itself collect either directly or through existing departments of the government, at home and abroad, pertinent information. Such information and data should be analyzed and interpreted by applying it to the experience of 'specialized trained research officials in the relative scientific fields (including technological, economic, financial and psychological scholars).'[9]

The first region he directed COI to examine, in September of 1941, was North Africa for intelligence gathering and analysis. Donovan, based on his travels, foresaw this region as a likely location for Allied military operations and any possible future North Africa operation would be a good testing ground of his fledgling intelligence organization and its capability to support modern military operations planning and execution.

COI Instructions for North Africa

As the branches of COI began working on its intelligence plan for North Africa, Donovan continued working behind the scenes with other government agencies to increase his/COI's access to other government organizations intelligence information and systems as outlined in COI's Charter. In August 1941, Wallace Banta Phillips, who was running a string of agents overseas in twelve countries as "K Organization", for the Office of Naval Intelligence, visited Donovan. Phillips offered his services and those of his organization's to Donovan. Donovan readily accepted and immediately started putting them to work in their current locations. Included among the agents already assigned to "K Organization" was Lieutenant Colonel (US Marine Corps Reserve) William A. Eddy, working in Egypt as the naval attaché.

Lieutenant Colonel Eddy was the son of American Presbyterian missionaries living in Syria, who was fluent in Arabic and the Arabic culture. He graduated from Princeton University and was commissioned in the Marines. He deployed for France with the 6th Marines in 1917, where he was wounded and returned to the United States and went on the inactive officer roster. In the meantime, Eddy was the president of Hobart College in upstate New York after having previously earned his doctorate in Philosophy at Princeton and honorary doctor of laws at St. Lawrence University and humane letters at Wooster College. He had also served for five years as the chairman of the English Department at the American University in Cairo, Egypt. In December 1940, Eddy had a chance encounter with the Marine Commandant, Lieutenant General Thomas Holcomb, where he volunteered his services. The Director of ONI, after talking to General Holcomb contacted Eddy and asked him, "How quickly can you report for duty?" He promptly resigned from Hobart, explaining to the college trustees, "College presidency is a job with which I am definitely out of love; I want to be a Marine!"[10] Within two months, Eddy went to Cairo, Egypt, this time as a naval attaché and a member of "K Organization". Once "K Organization" moved under COI, Donovan quickly made Lieutenant Colonel Eddy his intelligence chief in North Africa. Eddy moved from Cairo to Tangier via London on September 14, 1941, to begin running the intelligence network.[*]

As Eddy was establishing his North African network, Donovan continued to work on President Roosevelt for operational action in North Africa. He presented plans to the President for undercover intelligence on October 10, 1941, and again on December 22, 1941, this time stressing the importance of subversive action, local resistance, and guerrilla-commando units to strategic planning.

> When he was asked to consolidate the undercover intelligence of G-2, ONI and COI in October 1941, therefore, he had a definite plan prepared. It was as he reported to the President, to station a COI representative at Tangier who could 'unify the activities of the vice consuls' and 'stimulate' their efforts [Lieutenant Colonel Eddy]. The representative would have official status for the security of

---

[*] Lieutenant Colonel Eddy was promoted to Colonel following the invasion and was promoted to the position of Chief of the OSS in the Mediterranean theater. In August 1944, he was released from active duty in order to accept an appointment as U.S. Minister to Saudi Arabia, where he served until July 1946. He died on 3 May 1962 in Lebanon at the age of 66 while serving as a consultant for the Arabian American Oil Company and was buried in Lebanon.

his activities, and a clandestine radio network would be established which could continue to operate in the event of a break in diplomatic relations; the use of diplomatic pouch and cable was set forth as essential to effective communications.

In his memorandum to the President of 22 December, Donovan indicated further the plans in which Eddy was briefed: 'That the aid of Native chiefs be obtained; the loyalty of the inhabitants be cultivated; fifth columnists organized and placed, demolition materials cached; and guerrilla bands of bold and daring men organized and installed.'[11]

These presentations and current information gathered from the vice-consuls and initial COI agents could only have further influenced Prime Minister Churchill and President Roosevelt's consideration for a North Africa invasion during their ARCADIA conference, December 22, 1941, to January 14, 1942, held in Washington D.C. During the conference, the prime minister and the president mulled over British and American combined action in North Africa. Their decision laid the foundation for planning Operation TORCH (known as Operation SUPERGYMNAST at the time) - the invasion of North Africa. This decision also gave COI the significant role of responsibility for secret and subversive activity in collaboration with the British SOE and SIS.[12]

On a brisk winter morning, shortly after the conference's conclusion, six weeks after Pearl Harbor, the President called Donovan to the White House and handed him COI's most substantive assignment so far. He tasked Donovan with the following actions in relation to the planning for action in French North Africa:

A. The twelve disciples [vice-consuls, already in French North Africa] were to serve, with Rooseveltian imprecision, under both Donovan and Robert Murphy.
B. FDR told his spymaster his principal task was, through secret arrangements with the French General Staff, to avoid the war between France and the United States that conceivably could follow an American invasion of French North Africa. Donovan was to find out which way the French colonials would jump if invaded-to the Allied side, to the Nazis, or would they hang on the fence.

C. Thirdly, he was to ensure that Spain remained neutral, for if it intervened during the period of the invasion, its army in Morocco might tip the scales in the favor of the Axis. Further, his agents were to determine if Generalissimo Franco intended to block Gibraltar and allow German troops to land from Spain into Spanish Morocco. If that happened, an invasion of North Africa would likely be doomed.

D. Donovan's agents had another North African assignment that further tested the nascent OSS's capacity for the clandestine. The organization was to invent diversions to mislead the Germans into thinking that, should an African invasion take place, it would occur at Dakar, on the continent's western bulge, fifteen hundred miles from the intended landing site.

E. Also, he was to ensure that the French fleet did not go over to the Germans and Italians.

F. To these ends Donovan was authorized to undertake large and expensive clandestine operations in concert with the British secret services.

G. To permit American political and intelligence representatives already in the main centers of French North Africa to keep Washington informed of the attitudes of the French Army and Navy, Donovan was to construct and lay a communications net embracing all the Mediterranean countries.

H. He was to arrange a secure system of providing financial assistance, and war stores when needed, to the elements within French North Africa that were prepared to neutralize French communications at the moment of invasion.

I. He was also to find ways and means of infiltrating the Atlantic islands, to establish whether they were being occupied by the Germans, in such a manner that he did not bring the Spaniards and the Portuguese out against the Allies. [13]

These tasks became the first outlined strategic level intelligence and operational requirements for the United States in the European Theater of Operations during World War II. The detail of the information required by the President would strain Donovan's organization quickly, but would also provide him and COI the first test of its capabilities prior to a major invasion of the European Continent. These directed tasks would also merge directly into the operational requirements needed by planners for possible military action. Donovan also realized that his fledgling organization was even more so now subject to great scrutiny from the established United States and British intelligence organizations. Operations in North Africa could be a great opportunity to quickly establish the roles and responsibility of COI and prove to these other intelligence organizations that Donovan / Murphy's men were more than adequate to the task.

COI in North Africa

In order to better understand the working relationship COI and Special Operations Executive (SOE), Donovan first consulted and worked with William "Intrepid" Stephenson to gain an agreement between Donovan and the British SOE as to which organization would have jurisdiction where.

> …the British and Americans began to dispute operational control of intelligence and special operations in North Africa. As the senior intelligence partner, the British wanted to be in charge. Donovan, however, insisted that North Africa should be an OSS operation. He noted that America would spearhead the invasion, that British nationals were banned from operating in North Africa, and that through the Murphy Weygand treaty America already possessed an existing intelligence network. Ultimately, North Africa was designated OSS turf in an agreement known as the Donovan-Hambro accords, which created a framework for conducting SOE and OSS special operations and defined British and U.S. operating areas. [14]

While the French had banned British nationals from working in French North Africa, the British had established a spy network in Algeria and French Morocco by leveraging intelligence capabilities of the exiled Polish Government in London. What Donovan did not know at the time and the British did not want to reveal, was that Agency Africa was operational and providing much of the intelligence COI was required to gather. The British Secret Intelligence (SI) and Special Operations (SOP) organizations in the Mediterranean region directed by Colonel Brian Clarke at Gibraltar agreed to be placed under COI jurisdiction specifically reporting to Lieutenant Colonel Eddy rather than expose Agency Africa. It now became Eddy's responsibility to report to London and Washington on all Allied and Axis information and activities occurring in French and Spanish North Africa.

Establishment of the OSS

Meanwhile, as all of this was occurring behind the front lines in North Africa, Donovan faced another fight among the various intelligence staffs across the United States Government. The struggle stemmed from issues over the Foreign Information Activities, which Donovan had created to begin the United States propaganda machine when COI was established.

> General Donovan raised the matter with the Joint Chiefs of Staff at a time when the general reorganization of information and intelligence agencies was pending. JCS proposed to the President, with General Donovan's concurrence, that COI be made the supporting agency of the JCS. (This would have happened at the time of COI's creation had the JCS existed. It was not established until January 1942, and the COI could not have been put under one service, whether the Army's G-2 or ONI.) North Africa presented an easily recognizable example of the manner in which the COI concept of secret intelligence, propaganda, morale, and physical subversion guerilla action could be used in preparing the way for a large-scale invasion. This constituted a cogent argument that OSS should be placed under the JCS when the COI was split into Office of War Information and OSS in June of 1942. North African operations were to be influential in the JCS decision when the continuance of OSS came into question later that year.[15]

It was decided by a combination of the Joint Chiefs and Donovan that COI should be transferred from the Executive Office of the President of the United States to the purview of the Joint Chiefs of Staff and redesignated the Office of Strategic Services (OSS). The directive separated the Foreign Information Activities Branch out from COI and transferred it to the Office of War. This occurred by Executive Order of June 13, 1942, while Donovan was in Europe. Now Donovan's organization was formally situated inside the military machine, which ultimately provided the necessary manpower, equipment, organizational and financial overhead needed to be effective for the prosecution of clandestine and intelligence gathering actions in support of military and diplomatic operations in the war against the Axis. To the COI members in the

Mediterranean region at this time, the organizational name change and shift under the Joint Chief's structure was transparent.*

As June 1942, ended, the twelve disciples had now been in the region for a year and their baseline of intelligence collection and activity was going to be tested. The OSS was operationally in charge of the advance force operations. With constant communication between Murphy and Eddy, the mutually supportive tasks established by the President were already underway. Nevertheless, once President Roosevelt decided to invade French North Africa on July 24, 1942, operations in North Africa gave Donovan the ultimate chance to prove the OSS' capability.

* In fact, COI asked the twelve disciples formally if they would like to become a member of COI, those that accepted were immediately incorporated into the organization and under the OSS were commissioned either to their Reserve rank or to the rank of Captain as a minimum.

[1] Thomas F. Troy. *Wild Bill and Intrepid Donovan, Stephenson, and the Origin of CIA.* New Haven: Yale University Press, 1996. 3.

[2] Perisco, *Roosevelt's Secret War,* 16.

[3] Thomas F. Troy. *Wild Bill and Intrepid Donovan, Stephenson, and the Origin of CIA,* 3.

[4] EE. UU. *War Report of the OSS.* New York: Walker, 1976. 6.

[5] Ibid. 6.

[6] Cline, *Secrets, Spies, and Scholars Blueprint of the Essential CIA,* 34.

[7] EE. UU. *War Report of the OSS,* 5.

[8] Smith, *OSS: the Secret History of America's First Central Intelligence Agency,* 1.

[9] Ibid, 7.

[10] Richard Camp, Jr., Leatherneck and Few Marines: Colonel William A. Eddy. *Leatherneck –Magazine of the Marines,* April 4, 2004. 12-13.

[11] EE. UU. *War Report of the OSS,* 94.

[12] Richard Dunlop. *Donovan, America's Master Spy.* Chicago: Rand McNally, 1982. 343.

[13] Perisco, *Roosevelt's Secret War,* 209.; Brown, Anthony Cave. *The Last Hero: Wild Bill Donovan : the Biography and Political Experience of Major General William J. Donovan, Founder of the OSS and "Father" of the CIA, from His Personal and Secret Papers and the Diaries of Ruth Donovan.* New York, N.Y.: Times Books, 1982. 217.

[14] Patrick K. O'Donnell. *Operatives, Spies, and Saboteurs,* 32.

[15] EE. UU. *War Report of the OSS,* xi.

CHAPTER 4

AGENCY AFRICA

> On 1 May, 1941, returning home from Tudor with London's radio message in my pocket, I knew that a new chapter in my life was about to begin. They had handed me an enormous task - total responsibility for building up an extensive network from scratch, in a vast territory, completely on my own, and in the shortest possible time.
> - Mieczysław Zygfryd Słowikowski, and John Herman. *In the Secret Service: The Lighting of the Torch*[1]

In July 1941, London sent a man to establish a clandestine intelligence network in French North Africa, based in Algeria. He did not officially violate the British and Vichy France agreement made in July 1940, which removed all British officials and intelligence personnel from France and its colonies after the attacks on the French fleet in July 1940. This man did not violate this agreement because he was in fact Polish, not British, and his government was not a party to the agreement. This man was to create an intelligence organization, whose members were mostly French and who crossed all level of colonial society from Army generals to stevedores and Arabs and all in between. According to its creator and lead agent of this organization, Agency Africa provided an immense wealth of intelligence information on all types of war related subjects in French North Africa from July 1941 to December 1942 contrary to the claims of the OSS records and personal memoirs by prominent characters in the planning and execution of Operation TORCH.

M.Z. "Rygor" Slowikowski was born at Jazgarzew near Warsaw (then part of Czarist Russia) in 1886. He joined a Polish military organization in his youth and fought in the Russo-Polish War of 1920. He graduated from the Higher Military Academy in 1925, and after serving on the Polish General Staff, worked on problems of organization and mobilization on the 1st Army Corps staff in Warsaw, at the Defense Ministry and as

Chief of Staff of the Frontier Defense Corps at Wilno (1934) and at Grondo (1936). In 1937, Slowikowski transferred to the Polish Foreign Office and was appointed Secretary at the Polish Consulate in Kiev, the capital of the Soviet Ukraine. His real role, however, was gathering intelligence on Southern Russia for the Second Bureau of the Polish General Staff.

After the invasion of Poland, he managed to reach France with his wife and young son where, under the *nom-de-guerre* "Dr. Dkowronski", he organized the evacuation of Polish troops left behind after the fall of France and helped set up an intelligence network inside of occupied France. In May 1941, the Polish Central Office in London ordered him to set up an intelligence network in French North Africa, which he did starting in July 1941. Slowikowski took the cryptonym "Rygor", which in English means rigorous, and his agency was code-named "Africa" (AFR). As a prudent measure in his own safety from "London Bureaucrats", though counter to his intelligence training, he kept a diary of his activities in the form of an enumerated register of messages and the cash book of the Agency's accounts. "Rygor" later used these notes to write his memoirs, *In the Secret Service: The Lighting of the Torch.* [2]

Establishment of Agency Africa

On July 21, 1941, "Rygor" arrived in Algiers. After his first few days in country, he received his first messages from London detailing information requirements needed by his new organization, which he had yet to establish. The Polish Intelligence "Central Office" requested he report on "the anti-aircraft defences in French North Africa (3511)

†; shipments of war materials to Germany and on the state of the Algerian railway network (3495); whether work had started in Dakar and if a 'hurdy-gurdy' (a two-way radio receiver) could be set up (3225), and what cover would the 'the Doctor' use (3502)."[3] These were the first of 1,244 messages "Rygor" received from London, from July 22, 1941, to November 12, 1942.

These messages, sent via radio from London to Agency Africa, pertained to all sorts of advance force intelligence requirements such as: ascertaining the conditions of specific French naval vessels in various ports, the types of defenses surrounding each of the ports along the Atlantic and Mediterranean coasts, types of raw materials being delivered to the German Armistice Commission, type and names of merchant vessels arriving and departing from the ports, to include their manifests and cargo holdings, and other such information. "Rygor" took these initial requests and based on his experience, created a list of the information requirements for his key agency heads to take note of and plan for as they began to use the agents they were recruiting.

> As this is the beginning of your Intelligence work, there are specific points that your future agents must pay special attention to, when reporting on the various armed services or different localities:
> 1. Agents must be made aware that when identifying *Army units*, the following information is requested:
>   a. Name of town of stationing garrison.
>   b. Name and number of the unit.
>   c. Size of the unit, with composition: regiments, battalions, companies and batteries.
>   d. Armaments. In the case of an artillery unit, the type: heavy, field, anti-aircraft, anti-tank, calibre of the guns and type of traction. Armoured units: weight of tanks and armoured vehicles.
>   e. Munitions: type and quantity.
>   f. Morale of the soldiers and their political orientation.
> 2. For *Air Force* identification, the following specifications are required:
>   a. Type and number of aeroplanes.

---

† The figures in brackets refer to the enumerated radio messages sent to and received from London.

      b. Stock of bombs, munitions and fuel.
      c. Hangars.
      d. Type of runways.
3. *Naval* assignments are divided into: navy, merchant marine and port. Until our naval expert arrives from Marseilles, the work should consist of monitoring the movements of ships in and out of ports. The numbers and names of vessels and all markings and names on sailors' caps should be noted. In case of *Merchant cargo*:
      a. Name of the ship.
      b. Time of arrival.
      c. From which port.
      d. Time of sailing.
      e. Destination.
      f. Cargo being loaded.[4]

Other specifics, such as type of armament, condition of crews on vessels, local populace actions and reactions to rumors of Allied invasion would also be tasked, but this base line provided each agent a quick start on how to be effective in their own area. "Rygor" correctly anticipated several messages and stated needs from the Central Office in London; however, his list details common sense items, needed by an advance force operation establishing an information baseline. It also gave "Rygor" and his lead agents a way to test the information coming from the agents before they were officially hired.

"Rygor" carefully established his intelligence network throughout French North Africa led by a small handful of Polish nationals, whom he had a longstanding friendship with, and more importantly by recruiting French North African men and women to gather the valuable information whether from the local police, government officials, miners, stevedores, doctors, shop keepers, Arabs, etc. Within only a few months, his agency provided a large amount of requested information back to London. During the month of November 1941 for example, "Rygor" radioed fifty-seven messages and received forty-eight. Among the more important information sent to London were:

Military: Further German transports at the airfield of El-Aouina (206); French military garrisons in Casablanca, Rabat, and Marrakesh (247); transfer of fighter aircraft group from Maison Blanche in Algiers to Sfax in southern Tunisia (248); Defence of Metline, guns calibre 340mm (210).

Naval: List of French naval units in Casablanca port 29.10.41 to 10.11.41 (220); military hydroplane base at Arzev to be increased by one wing 12 hydroplanes (223); Oran ship movements (224) Oran list of ships in port (225); Oil tanker SS *Le Tarn* reported by message 172 on 23.10.41 to sail from Oran to Bizerta to Tripoli was torpedoed by British submarines and is being repaired in port of Algiers (231 and 238); German transporters in Tunisian territorial waters (201); Sinking of transporter carrying German Afrika Korps unit 135 (198).

Various: Transfer of interned British airmen to the camp at Laghouat (212); Transport of flour from Tunisia to Libya (200); Increase of German 'tourists' in Algeria and opening of 'German centres' to be known as consulates in Casablanca, Algiers and Tunis (234).

As a routine precaution, Central Office [London] required confirmation of many of our previous messages, also additional information regarding Bizerta port and Tunis airfield which appeared to be of very special concern for them.[5]

The level of detail provided in these reports was the same throughout the Agency's existence. "Rygor" took the time to not only receive and transmit the data, but also to analyze it for gaps in the information and redirect his agents as necessary to fill in the missing details.

Despite the amount of active French and German counterintelligence in French North Africa, "Rygor" and his associates were able to continue to provide detailed level of information directly to London at all times. However, early in October 1941, "Rygor" suspected the presence of another Allied Intelligence Service working in the area. "Rygor" inquired with London if he could contact the representative. London responded that they did not have any representative there (4932)."[6]

Contact with the Americans

What London did not tell them was there was an effort by the Americans to have an intelligence presence in the region as well. This became readily apparent to "Rygor" by his agents as they worked in their respective areas. Agency Africa became aware of the twelve vice-consuls in the region soon after "Rygor" arrived in late July 1941. "Rygor's" arrival was within a week or so of the remaining vice-consuls arrival into the region. "Rygor" then ensured the American Consulate's personnel were watched to ensure that they were not working the same agents as his organization. "Rygor" and his agents realized that "from the Intelligence standpoint, we were wasting our time as they were behaving as diplomats really should behave!"[7]

"Rygor" made his first contact with the American vice-consul John Knox shortly after Hitler declared war on the United States on December 11, 1941. The initial contact was made through a third party and agreed to by Knox. "Rygor" then went to the American Embassy in Algiers to assess its intelligence apparatus and information gathered. Upon his arrival, he found that the Americans were very polite and well mannered, but lacking in information about key areas around the region. To "Rygor", this only reinforced the fact that they acted like diplomats. Asked if the vice-consuls could help him in any way, "Rygor" and John Knox and his partner vice-consul John Boyd initially agreed to send "Rygor's" intelligence documents through American Diplomatic Pouches to London. This would allow Agency Africa bulk information to leave French territory without intervention from the Germans and French based on the agreement between Mr. Murphy and General Weygand made nearly a year earlier.

"Rygor" first began to make use of this arrangement on January 2, 1942, but on his second pouch drop off, the request was made to have the contents unsealed for inspection by the vice-consuls based on a requirement from Lieutenant Colonel Eddy as he established his position in Tangier as the head of the OSS operations. "Following

Eddy's arrival, all intelligence secured by the operatives in North Africa was routed to

him by pouch and radio."[8] "Rygor's" response to this was:

> Having no other alternative, I was compelled to agree. I well realized that, by
> handing the vice-consuls our unsealed pouch, they could exploit the fruits of our
> labour by copying our information and sending it directly to Washington. I
> resigned myself to writing it off as a payment to the Yanks for the service they
> were more than willing to perform for us. Information gathering was our primary
> task; in reality, it was unimportant whether London or Washington obtained it
> first. [9]

This arrangement obviously allowed Lieutenant Colonel Eddy and OSS to began

exploiting Agency Africa's work for their own analysis and use – yet, as the consolidator

of all information for the Allies in the region, it was Eddy's right to look and report

accordingly.

On February 6, 1942, Mr. Murphy invited "Rygor" to meet him after delivering

his next pouch. At this meeting, Murphy acknowledged the wealth of information

submitted by Agency Africa. "Rygor" states, "I had no objection to that, provided they

[Washington] were informed that their source was Intelligence Service Agency Africa of

the Polish Army in North Africa." Murphy, who never mentions his contact with

"Rygor" in his memoirs, responded to "Rygor" by saying, "Naturally it is understood that

this is part of our gentlemen's agreement!" [10]

Over the course of the next five months, according to "Rygor", he delivered his

pouches to the American Embassy routinely and openly acknowledged that Washington

and London used the information contained inside them. As the decision continued to

develop to execute the invasion of French North Africa, the information requirements for

planning grew as well. "Rygor" continued to provide his information to London and

Eddy and had meetings with Mr. Murphy and Lieutenant Colonel Eddy. These meetings revealed to "Rygor" that Murphy and Eddy knew much of the information requirements in the region based on the exploitation of the pouches and the vice consul and OSS agents, but lacked some specific details that "Rygor's" agents had gathered and he sent via radio to London.

Murphy and Eddy along with "Rygor" held one of most important of these meetings in early August 1942, just prior to their departures to Washington and London to brief the President, Joint Chiefs, and Allied planners with current information on the conditions and sentiments of the French in North Africa. The conference discussed the military, economic, and diplomatic situation in French North Africa based on the information complied and analyzed among the three of them by their respective intelligence networks. According to William Langer, who compiled the report on the diplomatic affairs associated with Operation Torch in 1944 and 1945, "Much had been accomplished in a few months, for which the colonel [Eddy] gave Murphy the chief credit. Intelligence had been greatly expanded, among the French, the Poles, and the Spanish Republicans."[11]

The End of Agency Africa

"Rygor" and Agency Africa continued to provide intelligence information to London and the vice-consuls through early November 1942. "Rygor" continued to analyze the questions coming from London and the information he transmitted back. He quickly deduced that the Allies were planning an invasion of some type in the near future. In late October 1942, he received confirmation of this from Boyd and Knox after delivering one of the pouches of information. The prospect of an Allied invasion only fueled the necessity to find the information required by London in order to make the invasion a success for the Allies.

Just before the invasion, the night of November 7, 1942, was a nervous one for "Rygor", his family, and close Agency Africa associates. They had put so much work and energy into gathering intelligence about the whole of French North Africa over the course of the past year and a quarter, that now they would see the fruits of their labor. On the morning of November 8, 1942, and for the next few days, "Rygor" maintained contact with London via radio and stayed out of the fighting and negotiations between the Allies and the French. Shortly after the fighting began, his agents went back to their normal lives, never contacted again. Their part in this operation was complete.

In late November, "Rygor" received word of his recall to London as soon as the situation settled and transportation could be arranged. "Rygor" returned to Britain in late December. During this trip to London "Rygor" discovered that he was really working for British Intelligence the entire time he was in Africa. The British used his Polish Army Intelligence Service Central Office to maintain a Polish face on the operation if the French ever questioned the British about the appearance of an Allied Intelligence service operating on French soil. "Rygor's" own intelligence agency cared little about the efforts he and his agency made in the course of just over a year. It was the British and the American's who rewarded "Rygor" once he returned to Algiers from London and officially closed down the Agency in early spring of 1943 as the Allies had destroyed Rommel's Afrika Korps and prepared for the invasion of Southern Europe.

The intelligence information provided by Agency Africa during the period of July 1941 and December 1942 was not discredited by any prominent member of the Allies in their preparation for Operation TORCH. However, other than a single sentence by William Langer in his book *Our Vichy Gamble,* about the diplomatic venture of Operation TORCH, there is no mention in any other memoir or biography or official record on the level of contribution by this organization. One possible explanation for this lack of acknowledgement by the OSS or vice consuls may be because the French Government does not want to acknowledge the fact that its own citizens provided the Allies with intelligence information when the Vichy Government had instructed otherwise. Another reason could be that COI/OSS was not as capable in collecting intelligence as "Rygor" had been and purposely led others to believe that the information collected came through OSS agents and informants, not Agency Africa. As the single primary source on the organization there must be some personal bias involved, much as can be expected about any memoirs written about or by "Wild Bill" Donovan and the origins of the OSS.

"Rygor's" memoirs tell a very different story from that of the OSS archives and memoirs of key participants in the Operation planning and execution. This study must add an additional question, does the appearance of another Allied intelligence network and its effectiveness to gather intelligence in French North Africa negate or merely change the dynamic of what intelligence and advance force capabilities the OSS was able to provide? [*]

[*] Rygor-Slowikowski was decorated on March 28, 1944 with the British Order of the British Empire and the American Legion of Merit. He attained the rank of Major General in the Polish Army and was demobilized in 1947. He later worked in a metal-polishing factory in England until age 70. Prior to his death, he writes his memoirs at the age of 92. He died at the age of 93 in 1989 in London.

---

[1] Mieczysław Zygfryd Słowikowski, and John Herman. *In the Secret Service: The Lighting of the Torch.* London: Windrush Press, 1988. 42.

[2] Ibid. xiii.

[3] Ibid. 62.

[4] Ibid. 68.

[5] Ibid. 92.

[6] Ibid. 79.

[7] Ibid. 81.

[8] EE. UU. *War Report of the OSS,* 94.

[9] Ibid. 106.

[10] Ibid. 117.

[11] William L. Langer. *Our Vichy Gamble.* New York: A.A. Knopf, 1947. 275.

CHAPTER 5

ANSWERING THE QUESTIONS

One special intelligence job that Browne and I did during the last few days of June and early in July was to clock the road from Tangier to Melilla through the Spanish Zone, since we knew that if any military operations were to take place in that zone, the armies would have to make use of that road. We kept a log of the road on the speedometer, noting to a tenth of a kilometer the location of all cuts, banks, overhangs, culverts, and bridges; in other words, all targets either for demolition or air attack; at the same time we noted the position of all visible Spanish defenses. Later this log was turned over to Colonel Johnson, who sent it to G-2.

- Carleton Stevens Coon, *A North Africa Story: The Anthropologist as OSS Agent, 1941-1943*[1]

The Establishment of the Networks

As has been discussed, each of the three organizations established their networks along different lines. The vice consuls arrived and performed much of their initial work themselves, or through local sympathizers. They set to work under Robert Murphy, acquiring maps, charting fields, measuring coastlines, sounding out French and Arab sentiment, watching ship movements, and trying to make up plausible stories for their superiors, the United States consuls, which would explain their frequent absences from their offices.[2] Much of their initial work was on their own, building a small network of local agents to support, but limited in scope and direction.

"Rygor" created Agency Africa using techniques he had learned while working in Russia and again in France smuggling Polish soldiers out of unoccupied France to Great Britain. He built his network to be completely clandestine, especially to his employees, unlike his American counterparts. He went so far as to establish himself as a businessman manufacturing and selling porridge. "Rygor" used the funds received from the business to offset his costs of running the network. After the invasion began, he impressed several of his employees, who then found out that he was the intelligence chief to whom they had been sending their information.

Many of the agents the Agency recruited provided information because they were pro de Gaulle and Free France, or they knew the information was against the Axis powers and thereby they were helping to free France from occupation. Agents were paid a small amount of money for the type and amount of information provided, but many were simply doing what they felt was right to be rid of the Germans. Over the course of the Agency Africa's existence, "Rygor" transmitted 1,244 of detailed information and analysis to London via one of two radios set up by his team. Six months after he started operations, "Rygor" established a reliable system, through the support of the Americans, to submit papers and non-time sensitive material to London.

When Lieutenant Colonel Eddy arrived in Tangier in December 1941, he set up his headquarters, formalizing the collection process with chains of informants to gather intelligence. Eddy connected with local resistance leaders and a religious brotherhood, based in Tangier, to use their networks of supporters to gather important intelligence on ports, landing beaches, and key military targets. Throughout 1941, these small groups gave valuable information to Murphy's "consuls".[3] Among his informants, he had a fisherman, who provided the location of antiaircraft guns and the movement of German submarines; herdsmen that located hidden fortifications; two coding clerks who turned over all decoded copies of German cables; an airline chief technician that passed on the blueprints of all airfields, their defenses and recognition signals. These agents and many others like them amassed a treasure trove of intelligence. Eddy also started to work with some resistance groups, who began to form in August 1940, in North Africa at Algiers,

58

Oran and Cherchell. They were small military or paramilitary cells, trying to gain

adherents in the army, among the staff, and in business circles in order to bring North

Africa back into the war. He used them not only for information, but also to smuggle

arms and equipment and organized the spread of subversive propaganda throughout the

region.

As directed, Lieutenant Colonel Eddy established his outstations using British

supplied radios and assigned each of them codenames: Casablanca became Lincoln;

Algiers, Yankee; Tunis, Pilgrim; Oran, Franklin; Tangier, Midway.[4] These radio stations

transmitted all intelligence information collected by the agents at the outstations to Eddy.

They also followed up with written records or information via diplomatic pouches. Once

Eddy received the information, he would analyze it and transmit the information and his

analysis to Washington and London. In the meantime, the men who ran these outstations

continued to watch shipping and cargoes, sketch defenses, and pass back their

information. Transmitting this data to Eddy allowed for centralized information flow

from the American agents out to the planners and senior leaders in Washington and

London. The short-term results were that British submarines frequently spotted and sunk

ships, whose movements the OSS men reported. The OSS provided other information

such as reports on the terrain around each of the proposed landing sites and others such

as:

> The defenses of Oran included forty-five fortified coastal guns of considerable
> strength; and of Arzew, six more. The most important of those on Djebel Santon,
> west of Mers el Kébir; on Djebel Murdjadjo, west of Oran; on Pointe Canastel,
> northeast of Oran; and on Cap Carbon, as the western edge of the Golfe d'Arzew.
> Fort du Santon had four 7.6-inch guns and a heavy concentration of antiaircraft
> artillery.

The Oran Division, estimated at 16,700, was stationed partly in barracks near the port and the main approaches to the city from southwest, south and east, and partly at inland stations within one day's march. The Army airfield at La Sénia, about six miles south-southeast of Oran, and a Navy airfield at Tafaraoui, twelve miles southeast, as well as a naval seaplane base at Arzew, twenty-two miles northeast of Oran, were part of the defense system. About one hundred combat aircraft were normally based there. Landing strips at Lourmel, Fleurus, Oggaz, and St. Denis-du-Sig supplemented the airfields. At the western extremity of the harbor of Oran, and at the naval base of Mers el Kébir, several French naval vessels were usually moored. [5]

Reports transmitted or sent with this much detail provided a very accurate picture to the planners in London and Washington. What Eddy did not know in his first few months in Tangier was that "Rygor" was also sending like information out via his radio network to London. However, there is no recorded complaint from the planners of any duplication of information. In fact, they kept that duplication a secret until Eddy learned of "Rygor's" operation.

The Questions

The biggest unknown for the Allied planners in preparation for the invasion of French North Africa was the French themselves. What would the French do if presented with an invading Allied army, whose purpose was to move through French North Africa, preferably unopposed, attack Rommel's army from behind, and secure the southern shore of the Mediterranean Sea for future operations in southern Europe? This complex question was uppermost in President Roosevelt's mind when he started his strategic advance force operations to answer the French question and other like questions for possible operations in French North Africa. In late 1940, he personally tasked Mr. Robert Murphy and Colonel William Donovan to provide situational understanding, area reconnaissance, an understanding of the key leaders, their general moods and attitudes of them and the people in the region. As 1941 started, both Murphy and Donovan were conducting their assessments in the Mediterranean region. President Roosevelt requested Murphy to find out "the extent of Weygand's real authority in Africa, what did the old soldier have in mind for the future, and what could the United States do to encourage him?"[6] The President requested Donovan to examine the economic, political and military aspects of the entire region. Their combined assessments based on the elements of national power looking at the diplomatic, information, military, and economic aspects of the Mediterranean region focused the President and his advisors on the regional issues and created an opportunity to look strategically at the area long before it became the object of diplomatic and military action.

As President Roosevelt made the decision to continue gathering intelligence in French North Africa, from the summer of 1941 through November 1942, the regional intelligence focus quickly shifted from strategic to operational and tactical information requirements. As planning activity and requirements increased the focus for information shifted from general information to specific in detail. Though unstated by either "Rygor" or OSS accounts, it appears that the two organizations split their information gathering responsibilities in French North Africa. Agency Africa remained focused entirely on the operational and tactical information requested by London, such as the continued information on troops, harbor information, ship movements, etc. "Rygor" stated that he maintained only limited contact with any resistance groups, primarily to collect their information and ensure the safety of his agents, who operated in their areas. This kept him out of the construction of insurgent groups and the diplomatic issues, which arose during the fighting.

The vice-consuls and OSS agents provided much of the same operational and tactical information initially as Agency Africa, but by their accounts, they continued to gather information regarding the resistance groups, the French leadership and the organization and coordination of these groups as well. Their focus was probably the most difficult based on the response of the key French leaders in the colonies. They also began to focus more on the operational aspects of advance force operations in physical preparation for the invasion.

The questions and tasks requested from London and Washington ranged from mundane in detail - measuring the height of the surf on Casablanca's beaches - to assessing which French leaders were pro-Allied and persuading the French military not to oppose an invasion.[7] Other, more political and population focused questions were given to the vice consuls and members of the OSS and Agency Africa like; which way would the French Army swing? Would it support the Allies invasion as a chance to start over in France's war against the Axis? Would the French offer limited resistance to regain their honor and then surrender in order to fight again? Would they resist any invasion at all costs and isolate themselves until the completion of the war?

The Operation TORCH planners and senior leaders not only wanted to know about French North Africa, but also about the intentions of Spain if the Allies were to make a move in North Africa. Commander Harry Butcher, Lieutenant General Eisenhower's aide-de-camp who kept a diary of all actions concerning the General, recorded on September 16, 1942, the day Mr. Murphy arrived in London to brief Eisenhower and the staff, "He couldn't answer the two big questions. 1. Would the Spaniards fight, especially in Spanish Morocco, and would they attempt to close the

62

Strait of Gibraltar or attack Gib[raltar] airdrome and harbor? 2. What would happen in France itself?"[8]

Some of the requests appeared a little more unusual to the agents on the ground. Carleton Coon, one of the vice-consuls in the Tangier Consulate, received one peculiar request from the SOE asking him to pick up typical stones along the roads in French Morocco in order to create tire-bursters in plaster of Paris to place along the roads to damage enemy vehicles. Coon states that he in fact did not find appropriate stones, but found that mule turds were plentiful and sent a few of these back instead. The Allies later effectively used these explosive turds in Tunisia against the Germans and Italians.[9]

London, who seemed to have a limited understanding of the full capabilities of Agency Africa at any one given time, tasked "Rygor" constantly with requests, which he was not fully prepared to answer at the time. For example:

> What were the possibilities of the French extending the Tunis-Gabés railway to the SE of Tunis and the Italians extending the railway from Tripoli to the west in the direction of Tunis? What had they accomplished and were there any preparations for laying tracks, constructing telephone lines, etc. in this territory? (3047).

> Other requests from Central Office were comparatively more 'straight forward' and included:
> Further details on the Tliananet oil well (3618); Information re trade with Japan, whether there were any Japanese ships in French North Africa ports and what were their cargoes (3160); the current strength of the coastal defences of Bizerta base and the port of Tunis which, according to the disarmament conditions were supposed to have been destroyed (3271); Tests were apparently being carried out on a new 46mm anti-aircraft gun in Sidi-bel-Abbes, report on the precise results of these tests (3521); Information required on heavy batteries at Casablanca (3384). [10]

"Rygor" states that he fulfilled most of the requests for information, even some of the more obscure requests. Some of them just took a little more time to collect.

Planners use of the Information

By the middle of July 1942, the Joint Intelligence Sub-Committee (JIC) in London submitted a memorandum on the possibility of a successful Allied cross-English channel invasion in 1942. The paper discussed three issues when issued on August 7, 1942,

> [T]he probable reaction of the forces of Vichy France; the threat to and through Spain; the form and extent of the other retaliation that might be expected from the Axis powers. Under each of these headings, it provided in support of its conclusions a mass of detail, which would be considered later on. Its general conclusion was as follows. The French Army and Air Force would resist in compliance with orders from Vichy to the point where they could *plead force majeure*; in the face of a resolute attack, they would probably collapse speedily. The French Navy would resist only in the Mediterranean; the Dakar-based force would probably not be involved.[11]

None of these conclusions would have been possible if the intelligence agencies in French North Africa had not provided the intelligence they had for an entire year prior to the agreement of the invasion. Additional requirements from the planners continued until after the ships had set sail from North America and Great Britain. For the intelligence networks, it was constant business. New requirements continued to stream in across the radios. Sometimes there was senseless timelines placed on the information from the planners, especially when they did not understand the amount of time it took to find the answers in a two-thousand mile desolate, desert region.

Some planners became a little skeptical as to the validity of some of the data. Was it totally objective, or did it have some bias on the part of the American agents to wish away some of the potential issues based on the agent's desire for an invasion to occur?

In the weeks that followed [the approval to execute Operation TORCH] the JIC appreciated the US diplomatic and intelligence organisations in north Africa, which produced most of the information …. But Washington had been sceptical of the enthusiastic reports it was receiving from its representatives in Algiers, and Whitehall, being more sceptical of them in view of the American determination to reduce the reach and weight of the Mediterranean assaults in order to allow for the Casablanca landing and guard against the threat from Spanish bases, had been reduced to such despair that doubt was cast on whether the *Torch* project should go forward.[12]

That healthy skepticism was warranted on behalf of the planners, but when combined with the reports from "Rygor", some of this detail was easy to confirm or deny. The other dilemma planners faced by not being physically present in the country or region was that they did not have that personal feeling of the situation and or the people involved. Since they were removed from the direct situation they had an objective look at the information, but there was some loss in understanding of the nuances of the people involved. For example, General Eisenhower states in his book, *Crusader in Europe,* that there was

> A constant stream of information came to us from consuls and other officials whom our State Department maintained in Africa throughout the war. All of this information was to the effect that in the regular officer corps of the French Army De Gaulle was at that time considered a disloyal soldier. His standing with the resistance elements of the civil population was vastly different. But at that moment resistance elements, particularly in Africa, were inarticulate and ineffective - and we had to win over the armed services as a first objective.[13]

Aware of the information and peculiarities involved with the French personalities, not only did Eisenhower and the planners have to plan for the military operation of the invasion itself, but they also work through plans on how to coordinate the resistance movements. This would consume much of Eisenhower's time, especially as the operation began and the negotiations for a quick settlement began as well. The agencies continued to respond to London and Washington on these questions and more. Three face-to-face meetings with the intelligence collectors, planners, and senior leaders of both Allied governments ultimately made the collected information worth something and provided everyone a clear understanding of what was happening in French North Africa.

Personal Briefs to the Planners and Executors

In late July 1942, Lieutenant Colonel Eddy went back to London to confer with the senior leaders and planners of Lieutenant General Eisenhower's staff. Before he left, Eddy, Murphy and "Rygor" held a conference at Murphy's special office on the Boulevard Sidi Carnot in Algiers to consolidate information and clear up some of the gaps that Eddy had.

> Eddy, who proved to have a good knowledge of our work, asked me for additional information to tie up his material. I explained to him that the gaps he had were because only our paper work went through the Americans. All the important and urgent reports were radioed directly to London. I was willing, however, to help him with his problems, and did not begrudge him several hours of my time, hoping that he would reciprocate by helping our men in need.
> Eddy's bosses in Washington required details of the military and economic situation in North Africa and, using the Agency's material, I discussed it with him at length. I also cleared up his queries concerning coastal defences, the equipment of army units and the morale of the French army.[14]

Armed with a consolidation of information needed to brief the senior leaders and planners in London from the two intelligence agencies working the issue, Eddy then departed for London, where he first met with Colonel Edward Buxton, the Assistant Director of OSS. Buxton arranged a dinner party at which Eddy met with Generals James Doolittle, George Patton, and George Strong, newly appointed chief of Army intelligence. Walking with a noticeable limp from his old leg wound, Eddy arrived in uniform, with five rows of ribbons over his left breast pocket, top row left to right, Navy Cross, Distinguished Service Cross, Silver Star with cluster and two Purple Hearts.

Patton gazed at the younger officer and exclaimed, "The son of a bitch's been shot at enough, hasn't he?"

Eddy detailed to these generals the amassed logistical data on tides, currents, depths of ports, locations of bridges, tunnels, and airfields, placements of coastal guns, the strength and deployment of French forces, and the most favorable landing sites. [15] He told about the French Army, the possibility of its nonresistance to a landing and of its support. He also provided a factual, detailed account of the French underground-- its strength, organization, leadership, and potential. He told of his own organization and of the intelligence on ship movements and defenses, which his group had already assembled. All three took particular note of Eddy's conclusion: "If we sent an expeditionary force to North Africa, there would be only token resistance."[16] This meeting lasted until early the next morning, when Major General Strong, impressed by what Eddy had to say, called General Eisenhower and arranged a meeting with him and Eddy.

The results of this meeting were obvious to Eddy when Eisenhower telegrammed the Army Chief of Staff, General George C. Marshall, saying, "Colonel Eddy of the U.S. Marines will arrive in Washington this week. He possesses much information which will be valuable to the Chiefs of Staff." In addition, Eddy gained from Eisenhower the planning insight that was ongoing in London and Washington, which spurred Eddy to create more defined plans for his organization and its support of the invasion. The result of these plans was greater involvement in the organizing and training of special forces to take over key points; the gathering of every conceivable piece of information about landing points; the smuggling out of Africa of various persons who might be useful to the

Allied plan; and the encouraging the German belief that the landings would take place at Dakar.[17]

On August 30 Murphy and General Marshall, Admiral Leahy, and Admiral Ernest King held the second important planning meeting. Murphy arrived to discuss the current state of affairs in French North Africa from a diplomatic position, just as Lieutenant Colonel Eddy completed his meetings with the same leaders and President Roosevelt.

> Robert Murphy, FDR's chief North African representative, reported to the President that what the French colonials wanted most was to be "complacently neutral. Far from wanting to be liberated, they just wanted to be left alone." But the wishes of the French were not Roosevelt's priority. On September 4, he secretly brought Murphy back to Hyde Park. The diplomat sensed the President's almost childlike delight in what he was about to divulge. Nearly 100,000 troops, the vast bulk of them American, he told Murphy, would land at twelve points stretching over a thousand miles from French Morocco to Algeria. [18]

Armed with the information that the invasion was going to happen, General Marshall felt it was necessary for Murphy to go to London to discuss his information and to become Eisenhower's Civil Military Affairs Officer. General Marshall thought it was best to send Murphy to London disguised as a lieutenant colonel, since in Marshall's words, "Nobody ever notices a lieutenant colonel."

Once Murphy arrived in London, he went immediately to see General Eisenhower and his senior staff. Eisenhower writes,

> From Mr. Murphy we learned the names of those officers who had pro-Allied sympathies and those who were ready to aid us actively. We learned much about the temper of the Army itself and about feeling among the civil populations. He told us very accurately that our greatest resistance would be met in French Morocco, where General August Paul Nogués was Foreign Minister to the Sultan. He gave us a number of details of French military strength in Africa, including information concerning equipment and training in their ground, air, and sea forces. From his calculations, it was plain that if we were bitterly opposed by the French, a bloody fight would ensue; if the French should promptly decide to join us we could expect to get along quickly with our main business of seizing Tunisia

68

and attacking Rommel from the rear. It was Mr. Murphy's belief that we would actually encounter a mean between these two extremes. Events proved him to be correct.[19]

Eisenhower further states that at the conference,

> Mr. Murphy gave most of us, particularly the Americans, our first vicarious acquaintanceship with a number of French officials. He discussed at length the characteristics and political leanings of the principal generals and the officials we were likely to encounter. He especially emphasized that at that time the American Government and people were held in high esteem by the French as compared to the antagonism that had developed toward the British.[20]

Murphy had obviously taken the time to develop not only his information, but after ten years of Foreign Service to France, he really knew most of the men he spoke of, their leanings, quirks, concerns, etc. This amount of detailed and relevant information convinced the senior leaders and planners that the information provided over the course of the past year was accurate enough to plan the invasion and subsequent operations against Rommel and his Afrika Korps.

The third meeting of significance occurred within a month of Murphy's return to Algiers. Major General Mast contacted Murphy to request an audience with the senior Allied commander in order to discuss potential opportunities with the French Forces in North Africa. On October 16, 1942, Murphy transmitted this message to Eisenhower. Eisenhower went to Prime Minister Churchill with the information and they agreed to send Major General Mark Clark, his deputy commander, to meet with Major General Mast on the coast of Algiers. On October 22, 1942, Clark and a small group met with Mast in a beach house outside of Algiers. During the conference, the opportunity opened to all French and American officers to pair off and discuss planning consideration in their individual areas. Clark's first task was to inform General Mast that the prospective landings would not be strictly American, though the Allies would exclude de Gaulle's Free French. Clark explained to Mast that because of the urgent demand for American naval forces in the Pacific, British air and naval forces would be required in the Mediterranean and, shortly after the landings, British ground troops to move eastward toward Tunisia. Mast made no objection to this.

To the surprise of the American officers, Mast and his staff had prepared plans on how the Americans could best invade North Africa, and the French handed their papers to Clark to take back to London. Except for the absence of an attack near Casablanca, their plans turned out to be almost identical to the plans already established for Operation TORCH. The Americans also learned that Mast's men controlled the Blida Airport at Algiers and the airfield at Bone and would make them available on the first day of the landings. Mast produced a detailed study of airfields, arsenals, batteries, and other key points, as well as a plan for the invasion, which, according to Allied Force Headquarters G-1 Colonel Julius C. Holmes, "surprisingly enough was almost identical with ours."[21]

In the end, this conference and those attended by Eddy and Murphy the previous months not only confirmed the information presented by the intelligence agencies throughout the past year to London and Washington, but renewed the confidence of all involved that their plans and understanding of the situation was accurate. This was indeed valuable, for the ships were already underway from Norfolk, Virginia, and various ports in Great Britain for their assault positions.

---

[1] Carleton Stevens Coon, *A North Africa Story: The Anthropologist As OSS Agent, 1941-1943*. Ipswich, Mass: Gambit, 1980. 26.

[2] Dulles, *Great True Spy Stories,* 382.

[3] Michael Kettle, *De Gaulle and Algeria, 1940-1960: From Mers El-Kébir to the Algiers Barracades [Sic]*. London: Quartet, 1993. 25.

[4] Dunlop, *Donovan, America's Master Spy,* 343.

[5] George F Howe, *Northwest Africa: Seizing the Initiative in the West*. Washington: Office of the Chief of Military History, Dept. of the Army, 1957. 48.

[6] Murphy, *Diplomat Among Warriors*, 73.

[7] Perisco, *Roosevelt's Secret War,* 210.

[8] Harry C. Butcher, *My Three Years with Eisenhower; The Personal Diary of Captain Harry C. Butcher, USNR, Naval Aide to General Eisenhower, 1942 to 1945*. New York: Simon and Schuster, 1946. 106.

[9] Coon, *A North Africa Story,* 31.

[10] Słowikowski, and Herman, *In the Secret Service: The Lighting of the Torch*, 164.

[11] F. H. Hinsley, and Michael Eliot Howard. *British Intelligence in the Second World War. Vol. II.* New York: Cambridge University Press, 1979. 464-465.

[12] Ibid. 470.

[13] Dwight D. Eisenhower, *Crusade in Europe*. Garden City, N.Y.: Doubleday, 1948. 83-84.

[14] Słowikowski, and Herman. *In the Secret Service: The Lighting of the Torch*, 176-177.

[15] Perisco, *Roosevelt's Secret War,* 215.

[16] Smith, *OSS: the Secret History of America's First Central Intelligence Agency,* 51.

[17] Stewart Johonnot Oliver Alsop, and Thomas Wardell Braden. *Sub Rosa; The O.-S.-S. and American Espionage*. New York: Reynal & Hitchcock, 1946. 88.

[18] Perisco, *Roosevelt's Secret War,* 210.

[19] Eisenhower, *Crusade in Europe*, 86-87.

[20] Ibid. 88.

[21] Blumenson, *Mark Clark,* 83.; Peter Tompkins, *The Murder of Admiral Darlan, A Study in Conspiracy*. New York: Simon and Schuster, 1965. 48.

CHAPTER 6

COMPARISONS

The President returned to Washington to find an OSS analysis that reinforced his intuition: North Africa made both political and military sense as America's debut into the European war. According to anti-Nazi colonial officers with whom Colonel Eddy met secretly, the French army would put up only token resistance against the invasion.
> - Joseph E. Perisco, *Roosevelt's Secret War.*

Did a fledgling American intelligence organization, the Office of Coordinator of Intelligence (later the Office of Strategic Services) accomplish all of the required advance force operation tasks as outlined in Department of Defense Joint Publication 3-02.1 *Joint Tactics, Techniques, and Procedures for Landing Force Operations* to ensure the success of the Allied invasion of French North Africa? The short answer is no, not by themselves. However, the total amount of tasks that the OSS accomplished is far greater than those it did not accomplish. Collectively, with the assistance of Agency Africa and Mr. Murphy and his vice consuls, the Allied intelligence collection and conduct of advance force operations in preparation of the invasion of French North Africa was a success.

The evidence suggests that there are two right answers on the intelligence information the OSS provided for planning the invasion. The OSS and Agency Africa both provided detailed intelligence information to both London and Washington. Yet, there is the issue of "Rygor" and John Knox agreeing to have Agency Africa's information open to the vice-consuls/OSS as it went to Lieutenant Colonel Eddy in Tangier. How much of the information did the OSS exploit for its own gain and how much was it shared as a partner in the overall objective of providing support to the mission? There are three possible answers to these questions. (A) The intelligence received from Agency Africa was fully incorporated into OSS messages sent to Washington and London as OSS gathered information. (B) The information received by the OSS was used to confirm or deny the OSS and vice consul collected information. (C) The information was combined with the OSS information and submitted as a consolidated report, with appropriate annotation as to who originated the information.

Without complete access to both sets of records, one can deduce that Eddy and his OSS agents could have used the information to confirm or deny OSS gathered information and or consolidate it with the appropriate credit to send to Washington and London. However, based on Eddy's own admission of his information gaps, most of which "Rygor" had submitted via radio and had not told Eddy, it is most likely that the information was taken, assimilated with OSS gathered information, and transmitted to Washington and London, but not credited to the gathering agency, which "Rygor" had asked to be done. In defense of Eddy's use of Agency Africa's information, as the collator and lead agent for intelligence information in North Africa, it was his duty to ensure duplication of sources and their information did not occur.

"Rygor", too, understood this and early on tried to ensure he was not duplicating efforts when he felt that there was another Allied intelligence agency at work in French North Africa. He made sure of this by contacting London, who told him that there was no other Allied agency at work in the area. It can only be deduced that "Rygor" was correct and that the other agency was the vice-consuls. However, with "Rygor" transmitting information without Eddy's knowledge it also provided London and Washington with two independent intelligence agencies collecting on the same information, thereby confirming the information given by each of the groups and possible exposing other information gaps needed for the planning process.

The use of "Rygor" and his intelligence information was a blessing for the OSS and Donovan, because it helped to establish quickly the usefulness of the OSS at a time when there were true questions about what this organization could provide. In May 1942, Donovan told Secretary of State, Cordell Hull that the war effort would suffer if these officers the vice consuls were not kept at their posts as intelligence observers. The War Department agreed.[1] The simple fact is that the information collected, analyzed and submitted to London and Washington was sufficiently accurate for planning and execution as detailed by the French themselves, when Major General Mast handed over the nearly identical plans to attack French North Africa created by his staff. But, as the history was written, Agency Africa was conspicuously left out in most cases.

Advance Force Information

The OSS and Agency Africa provided all of the intelligence and operational information required by the definition of Advance Force Operations under the Supporting, Advance Force, and Pre-assault Operations Paragraph. Each of the organizations provided hydrographic reconnaissance. This included; sea state information, depths of the ports, any obstacles and defensive systems at the ports, amount of sea traffic in the region, French and German fleet activity and knowledge of any unusual conditions based on historical precedent and local populace information. The OSS even went so far as to provide two harbor pilots for the invasion force.

> … on September 15, an aircraft touched down and rolled to a halt at one end of the field. Two figures in unkempt clothing deplaned and glanced around nervously. Two men hustled them to a little-used hangar, where the group was

joined by two young Americans - operatives in Colonel 'Wild Bill' Donovan's OSS.

The two arriving passengers were known by fictitious names and carried false identity papers furnished by the OSS. Their real names were Carl Victor Klopet and Jules Malavergne, and they represented the fledgling American agency's biggest coup to date. They had been smuggled out of French Morocco by the OSS to play crucial roles in Operation Torch.

Carl Klopet had lived in Casablanca for many years, and his work in the marine salvage business had given him intimate knowledge of ports, beaches, and coastal defenses along the entire French Moroccan shoreline. Jules Malavergne had been a ship's pilot on the Sebou River at Prot Lyautey for 20 years and knew every shallow, sandbar, and twist in the river channel.[2]

This action by Eddy made General Eisenhower angry. He had not authorized this action and when notified by General Marshall of its occurrence he demanded to know why the OSS had taken this action without his approval. A short investigation revealed that the project had been eagerly approved by Major General Patton, who had neglected to inform Eisenhower's staff. These two men went on to accompany the landing forces and guide them safely to the selected landing points and around several of the harbor defenses in their respective areas.

As the time of the invasion drew closer, the landing beaches and seaward approaches were prepared as required. Part of General Clark's mission in October 1942, was to confirm the information already given about the beaches. His rendezvous with Murphy and General Mast was a good test of the information and the systems in place for the OSS agents to bring in the rest of the invasion force. On the morning of the actual invasion OSS agents, waiting to greet the troops on certain beaches, handed them French military maps and guided them inland. The enemy was where these agents said it would be, armed as predicted and in the numbers estimated.[3]

In the area of reconnaissance and surveillance of advance force objectives, landing beaches, landing zones, drop zones, and high-speed avenues of approach into the landing area, there was a wealth of information provided by both groups. "Rygor" details in his memoirs the multitude of reports and the information contained. Each of his agents received a thorough outline of information to be observed and reported. Both Murphy and Eddy received and detailed the same type of lists. The vice consuls had also acquired maps, chart fields, measure coastlines, sounded out French and Arab sentiment, and watched ship movements prior to and after Eddy's arrival. Based on the amount of detail Eddy briefed to the generals in London and Washington, they were more than impressed with Eddy and the amount of information and analysis he presented. They confirmed for him that the intelligence collected was more than sufficient to ensure the planners knew the accuracy of the information they had received. Even Murphy had performed his part in the data collection as he discussed the details of the road from Oran to Casablanca on September 17, 1942, with Commander Butcher:

> In the discussion with Murphy last night and this morning, I had asked him about this route [overland route from Casablanca to Oran]. He said there is a sixteen-foot macadam road from Oran to Casablanca. He had driven it in ten hours without pressing. The railway is antiquated and could move only 1500 tons a day - about enough to supply one division. The railway can be rehabilitated by our engineers. It is standard gauge. Murphy said that he had caused an inspection of the roadbed and found it satisfactory.[4]

The vice consuls collected the information required, especially if they were picking up rocks and donkey turds for use in Tunisia. Murphy too had done his part and with the details he was able to provide regarding the political and diplomatic situation involving the French leadership in North Africa he truly had done his homework prior to giving the information to the generals and their staffs.

The last portion of the task of reconnaissance and surveillance of advance force objectives is determining if the required conditions for the assault have been established. As the assault force came over the horizon to their landing beach areas and the paratrooper aircraft headed for their drop zones, the last messages out were from Eddy and Murphy stating that all was ready. The conditions for the invasion had been met. Operationally the resistance forces were attacking and in control of large areas for a time during the night of the invasion and all of the planning intelligence information was already given. Only the absolute last minute detail of the final enemy disposition in certain incidences was not known. Yet, as already described, the OSS agents were on certain beaches with maps and enemy disposition as the Allied forces came ashore. "Rygor" states that he remained alert for the next few days of the invasion monitoring his radio system, but staying out of the fighting and diplomatic struggles.

By breaking down the requirements of Advance Force Operations with an emphasis on the Supporting, Advance Force and Pre-assault Operations, one can conclude that the OSS did in fact provide the support needed prior to and during the invasion. The OSS, combined with Agency Africa, provided the accurate information needed for the invasion force to be successful. Nonetheless, Agency Africa's involvement was information collection and not the physical support as required to assist the invading force.

The President's Requirements

In addition to advance force operations, the President tasked Donovan to provide other actions and information. These nine requirements were given to Donovan at their meeting post the ARCADIA Conference in 1942. They outlined clearly what President expected the OSS to accomplish. Of these nine requirements, the first and sixth

requirements were directives. Of the remaining seven requirements, the OSS fully

accomplished the following three tasks:

> C. Thirdly, he was to ensure that Spain remained neutral, for if it intervened during the period of the invasion, its army in Morocco might tip the scales in the favor of the Axis. Further, his agents were to determine if Generalissimo Franco intended to block Gibraltar and allow German troops to land from Spain into Spanish Morocco. If that happened, an invasion of North Africa would likely be doomed.

> D. Donovan's agents had another North African assignment that further tested the nascent OSS's capacity for the clandestine. The organization was to invent diversions to mislead the Germans into thinking that, should an African invasion take place, it would occur at Dakar, on the continent's western bulge, fifteen hundred miles from the intended landing site.

> G. To permit American political and intelligence representatives already in the main centers of French North Africa to keep Washington informed of the attitudes of the French Army and Navy, Donovan was to construct and lay a communications net embracing all the Mediterranean countries.

Donovan and the OSS accomplished Requirement C by infiltrating the Spanish Embassy

in Washington and stealing the diplomatic cipher codebooks. This allowed the United

States the opportunity to read Spanish diplomatic messages and predict Franco's reaction

to any action by the United States or its Allies in the region.

The OSS accomplished Requirement D by continuing a strong psychological and

information operations campaign, as General Kesselring, who was the German

commander in North Africa over Rommel, states:

> My Reflections on the Objective of the Allied Invasion of November 1942. My Countermeasures.
> The American invasion was preceded by propaganda, which I must classify as a most effective war of nerves. For weeks the most contradictory rumors, opinions, and observations were channeled to my headquarters. Information on the invasion site, strength of landing forces, and equipment were fabricated. Fleet movements off the west coast of Africa led me to guess on the most widely different landings

there. The large and growing enemy concentration at GIBRALTAR pointed toward an invasion along the Mediterranean coast; the various positively identified aircraft carriers and large transport vessels pointed toward a large-scale landing at a location out of range of air support based on GIBRALTAR, MALTA, ALEXANDRIA, and Syria. Ships repeatedly putting to sea from GIBRALTAR were bound to increase the uncertainty as to the start of operations for half a day at a time. As a result of the critical examination of all reports and messages I reasoned in the following manner:

(1). There will probably be a connection between the strategy involved in the invasion and that involved in the moves of the British Eighth Army in Africa. A landing on the west coast of Africa is therefore unlikely.

(2). This invasion is a virgin operation. The enemy lacks experience. American army units are not battle tried.

The Allies know that there are Axis aerial formations in considerable strength based in Italy and her islands. These formations can not be neutralized by pursuit formations launched from carriers. In addition, the Allies know that there is still the Italian Fleet to be reckoned with. That fleet is still intact. Operating with the Air Force in the vicinity of Allied -held ports it can make its presence felt in a rather unpleasant manner.

For this reason, landings to close to the Italian islands and coastline can safely be considered as unlikely. A breakthrough along the narrow strait between Sicily and TUNIS is, therefore, out of the question. This eliminates the possibility of a landing at TRIPOLI and BENGASI, which would otherwise have been very likely.

If the enemy lands on the coast of North Africa, he will enjoy security by virtue of the distance between the invasion site and Axis airdromes on Sicily and Sardinia. In order to attack the Allied beachhead our bombers and torpedo planes will be forced to fly maximum distances. This fact is to the advantage of the invasion fleet. It means a decrease in the number of expected Axis air raids and in the bomb load dropped. Damaged Axis planes will find the long return flight extremely risky. The Italian fleet, of course, can not be counted upon to leave its home ports and sail long distances in order to seek out and engage to Allied fleet.

Algeria must be considered as invasion area. Just how much the French are going to resist is a moot question. Even the slightest resistance will help our cause.

The road to Tripolitania, or for that matter, to TUNIS, is long, but there are certain advantages in this fact as far as the initial Allied maneuvers are concerned.

On the very day of the Allied landing in North Africa, the Reich Marshal, speaking for himself and Hitler, declared my estimate of the situation to be incorrect. He told me that the opinion prevailed at Hitler's Headquarters that southern France was the target. He informed me that I was to be responsible for the commitment of the entire Air Force strength under my command against this landing.

Signed Kesselring[5]

Mission accomplished for the OSS and the Allies. Though Kesselring was not fully persuaded that Dakar was the intended objective, he and Hitler's Headquarters was not prepared for the landings when and where they happened.

Lieutenant Colonel Eddy and the OSS five established radio outstations accomplished President Roosevelt's Requirement G. This allowed the continuous communications within the region and with London and Washington. In addition to the radios, the OSS used diplomatic pouches to send their information to London and Washington. This complete network allowed much of the detailed information to be delivered securely to the planners in both capitals.

The following four tasks were not completely accomplished by the end of the invasion.

B. FDR told his spymaster his principal task was, through secret arrangements with the French General Staff, to avoid the war between France and the United States that conceivably could follow an American invasion of French North Africa. Donovan was to find out which way the French colonials would jump if invaded-to the Allied side, to the Nazis, or would they hang on the fence.

E. Also, he was to ensure that the French fleet did not go over to the Germans and Italians.

H. He was to arrange a secure system of providing financial assistance, and war stores when needed, to the elements within French North Africa that were prepared to neutralize French communications at the moment of invasion.

I. He was also to find ways and means of infiltrating the Atlantic islands, to establish whether they were being occupied by the Germans, in such a manner that he did not bring the Spaniards and the Portuguese out against the Allies. [6]

Of the tasks not fully accomplished, Requirement B was probably the hardest to accomplish by the OSS and was perhaps their largest failure. The previous attacks by the British on the French fleet and attacks in Dakar and Syria left a sour taste in the mouths of most French Officers. Murphy, Eddy, and "Rygor" were very conscious of this fact and reported it on several occasions. The prediction of the events of the first days of the invasion were not pure speculation, but nor were they pure fact. General Eisenhower records Murphy's attempt to help the military leaders understand the political and military situation in French North Africa during the September 1942 planning conference in London.

> From Mr. Murphy we learned the names of those officers who had pro-Allied sympathies and those who were ready to aid us actively. We learned much about the temper of the Army itself and about feeling among the civil populations. He told us very accurately that our greatest resistance would be met in French Morocco, where General August Paul Nogués was Foreign Minister to the Sultan. He gave us a number of details of French military strength in Africa, including information concerning equipment and training in their ground, air, and sea forces. From his calculations it was plain that if we were bitterly opposed by the French a bloody fight would ensue; if the French should promptly decide to join us we could expect to get along quickly with our main business of seizing Tunisia and attacking Rommel from the rear. It was Mr. Murphy's belief that we would actually encounter a mean between these two extremes. Events proved him to be correct. [7]

Eddy and Murphy reported to the generals and the President that there would be token resistance against the Allied invasion force. This was the case, although the President told Donovan to avoid war with the French. The OSS did not accomplish this task, unfortunately for the 1,400 Allied and 700 French troops who died in the three days of fighting.

The OSS did not fulfill Requirement E not because of its actions, but because of Murphy and the negotiations between Eisenhower, Clark, and Admiral Darlan as to the status of the French fleet. Admiral Darlan ordered the fleet commander to give control of the ships to the Allies, but he in turn scuttled the fleet in port. This was not Churchill or Roosevelt's intended action by the French, but it was a way to ensure that neither the Allies nor the Axis gained control of the fleet.

In order to accomplish Requirement H, Eddy and Murphy through Donovan attempted to secure arms, money, and equipment for the resistance forces in the region from the Joint Chiefs. Even though the President outlined these requests, the Joint Chiefs felt that any support to the resistance would cause a shortfall in the amount of equipment available to the invasion force. However, the point was made by General Marshall that the amount required was equal to that of a complete United States infantry division and the United States could not even outfit its own units adequately to conduct the invasion.

Lastly, Donovan attempted to complete Requirement I. He had an agent visit the Atlantic Islands, but he was never able to firmly establish if the Germans had in fact occupied these islands. Donovan also used his agents in Spain and Portugal along with intercepts of Spanish diplomatic messages in order to gain situational awareness on the intentions of these governments in regards to the islands, but the information gathered became inconsequential to the whole operation as time went on.

Conclusion

If a comparison is made of the requirements tasked to requirements completed, whether directed by the President or to be conducted through doctrine, then the OSS does not deserve the accolades so many offered the organization at the conclusion of the invasion.

However, the actual requirements completed by the OSS had major impact on the entire operation. Yet without the support of Major "Rygor" Slowikowski and his Agency Africa, and Mr. Murphy and his vice consuls, the entire affair could have been much deadlier for both sides.

Much has been discussed about Colonel Donovan and his goals for the OSS. Ultimately he wanted his new organization to succeed in supporting the United States and its Allies against the threat of fifth column actions against America. He also strove for the OSS to provide strategic and operational intelligence to the President and senior government leaders, which was so woefully neglected in between World War I and 1941. Unfortunately the creation of the COI was too late to affect the Japanese actions at Pearl Harbor, but his fledgling organization now had a chance to quickly make a difference in French North Africa. However, it has been said that,

> Donovan welcomed the attack [invasion of North Africa] as a means of demonstrating the OSS's usefulness: he aligned himself with the positive strategic assessment of the operation's potential; he promised that the OSS would through clandestine maneuvers persuade the majority of the Vichy French not to resist the American landings; he predicted that OSS guerilla and sabotage teams would smooth the way for the advancing regular soldiers, minimizing casualties and helping the Allies to establish a North African foothold with relative ease.

> But Donovan's optimism and promotional instincts had run away with him. OSS sabotage operations were not sufficiently effective to offset certain shortcomings in the Allies' military planning. Far from passively accepting the American invasion, the Vichy French fought it, giving the Nazis time to mass their forces to the east in Tunisia. Within three days, 1,400 Americans and 700 Frenchmen lay dead. At this point, the Allies deemed it prudent to strike a deal with Adm. Jean Darlan, a Vichy officer hitherto noted for his collaboration with the Germans. This deal stopped the Vichy resistance, but the American presence in North Africa had been purchased at a cost of American lives and principles.[8]

Donovan's persistence coupled with President Roosevelt and Prime Minister Churchill's insistence at making French North Africa a good place to open a second front drove many to look at the actions of the OSS as an operational proving grounds and a chance for Donovan to prove his concept and organization capable of doing what they advertised.

This was the first time the OSS had performed its intelligence collection and operational support tasks. The mistakes made and the requirements which were not completed are much of what was to be expected in any military operation. The fact remains that first, under the guidance and control of Mr. Murphy and then jointly under Murphy and Lieutenant Colonel Eddy, the vice consuls and agents of the OSS learned while on the job of collecting information and preparing for the invasion within a year and a half. Fortunately for the Allies, the British choose a talented man in Major "Rygor" Slowikowski to establish and operate an intelligence network outside of the vice consuls and OSS. I contend that without his support, much of the operational planning requirements would not have been met as timely or as detailed and Operation TORCH would have sustained even more casualties on both sides.

Advance force operations include reconnaissance, overt and covert operations to shape the battlespace and preparation of the invasion area prior to the first landings. The OSS performed these actions and requirements well. Men were on the beaches at the right time and place, maps were handed out describing the enemy disposition, and the French military and civil leaders were engaged by Mr. Murphy to quickly stop any and all fighting in the colonies. The reconnaissance and intelligence information gathered was sent to London and Washington in a timely manner for planners and executors to create the invasion plans and execute effectively. When Major General Mast handed over his staff's plan on how to invade to Major General Clark, the closeness to the Allied plan could have only come from the same level of information passed. The confidence in the information was questioned at several points throughout the nearly two years spent gathering intelligence in the region. However, each time many if not all of the questions were answered to satisfaction or the invasion would not have happened.

In war, there is no perfect amount of intelligence. There was no prediction possible for the actions of some leaders and men at the local level when their home is invaded. Unfortunately, 1,400 Allied and 700 French soldiers and sailors died before terms were agreed to and the cease-fire was given on both sides.

Operation TORCH was the first time America fought in the European Theater of Operations on a large scale. It started in late 1940 and ended with the destruction of Rommel's Afrika Korps in May 1943. This was a time for many intelligence firsts to be accomplished; the establishment of the OSS and Agency Africa and the use of American diplomats to conduct covert intelligence collection, for example. There was no perfect concept or scheme on how all of this was to be done. However, when the soldiers and sailors of the United States and Great Britain invaded French North Africa on November 8, 1942, these agencies provided more than enough intelligence information to conduct combat operations against a somewhat resistant opponent. Like the OSS, this invading army was new and did not handle itself perfectly either. There were many lessons learned, however, the invasion was accomplished and preparation for movement against Rommel and his Afrika Korps could begin.

---

[1] Smith, *OSS: the Secret History of America's First Central Intelligence Agency,* 46.

[2] William B. Breuer, *Operation Torch: The Allied Gamble to Invade North Africa.* New York: St. Martin's Press, 1985. 53.

[3] Perisco, *Roosevelt's Secret War,* 215.

[4] Butcher, *My Three Years with Eisenhower,* 111.

[5] Donald S. Detwiler, Charles Burton Burdick, and Jürgen Rohwer. *World War II German Military Studies: A Collection of 213 Special Reports on the Second World War Prepared by Former Officers of the Wehrmacht for the United States Army: a Garland Series.* New York: Garland Pub, 1979. 77-81.

[6] Perisco, *Roosevelt's Secret War,* 209.; Brown, *The Last Hero,* 217.

[7] Eisenhower, *Crusade in Europe,* 86- 88.

[8] Rhodri Jeffreys-Jones. *Cloak and Dollar: A History of American Secret Intelligence.* New Haven: Yale University Press, 2002. 147-148.

BIBLIOGRAPHY

Books

Alsop, Stewart Johonnot Oliver, and Thomas Wardell Braden. *Sub Rosa; The O.-S.-S. and American Espionage.* New York: Reynal & Hitchcock, 1946.

Ambrose, Stephen E., and Richard H. Immerman. *Ike's Spies: Eisenhower and the Espionage Establishment.* Garden City, N.Y.: Doubleday, 1981.

Atkinson, Rick. *An Army at Dawn: The War in North Africa, 1942-1943.* New York: Henry Holt & Co, 2002.

Blumenson, Martin. *Mark Clark.* New York: Congdon & Weed, 1984.

Breuer, William B. *Operation Torch: The Allied Gamble to Invade North Africa.* New York: St. Martin's Press, 1985.

Brown, Anthony Cave. *The Last Hero: Wild Bill Donovan : the Biography and Political Experience of Major General William J. Donovan, Founder of the OSS and "Father" of the CIA, from His Personal and Secret Papers and the Diaries of Ruth Donovan.* New York, N.Y.: Times Books, 1982.

Butcher, Harry C. *My Three Years with Eisenhower; The Personal Diary of Captain Harry C. Butcher, USNR, Naval Aide to General Eisenhower, 1942 to 1945.* New York: Simon and Schuster, 1946.

Calvocoressi, Peter. *Top Secret Ultra.* New York: Pantheon Books, 1980.

Camp, Richard Jr. Leatherneck and Few Marines: Colonel William A. Eddy. *Leatherneck –Magazine of the Marines,* April 4, 2004. 12-13.

Cline, Ray S. *Secrets, Spies, and Scholars Blueprint of the Essential CIA.* Washington: Acropolis Books, 1976.

Coggins, Jack. *The Campaign for North Africa.* Garden City, N.Y.: Doubleday, 1980.

Coon, Carleton Stevens. *A North Africa Story: The Anthropologist As OSS Agent, 1941-1943.* Ipswich, Mass: Gambit, 1980.

Detwiler, Donald S., Charles Burton Burdick, and Jürgen Rohwer. *World War II German Military Studies: A Collection of 213 Special Reports on the Second World War Prepared by Former Officers of the Wehrmacht for the United States Army : a Garland Series.* New York: Garland Pub, 1979.

Dulles, Allen Welsh. *Great True Spy Stories.* New York: Harper & Row, 1968.

Dunlop, Richard. *Donovan, America's Master Spy.* Chicago: Rand McNally, 1982.

Edwards, Harry W. *A Different War: Marines in Europe and North Africa.* Marines in World War II commemorative series. Washington, D.C.: History and Museums Division, Headquarters, U.S. Marine Corps, 1994.

Eisenhower, Dwight D. *Crusade in Europe.* Garden City, N.Y.: Doubleday, 1948.

Foot, M. R. D. *SOE An Outline History of the Special Operations Executive 1940-46.* London: British Broadcasting Corporation, 1984.

Funk, Arthur Layton. *The Politics of TORCH; The Allied Landings and the Algiers Putsch, 1942.* Lawrence: University Press of Kansas, 1974.

Hinsley, F. H., and Michael Eliot Howard. *British Intelligence in the Second World War.* New York: Cambridge University Press, 1979.

Hinsley, Francis Harry. *British Intelligence in the Second World War: Its Influence on Strategy and Operations. Vol. 1.* London: H.M.Stat.Off, 1979.

Howe, George F. *Northwest Africa: Seizing the Initiative in the West.* Washington: Office of the Chief of Military History, Dept. of the Army, 1957.

Jeffreys-Jones, Rhodri. *Cloak and Dollar: A History of American Secret Intelligence.* New Haven: Yale University Press, 2002.

Jeffreys-Jones, Rhodri, and Andrew Lownie. *North American Spies New Revisionist Essays.* Modern war studies. Lawrence, Kan: University Press of Kansas, 1991.

Kettle, Michael. *De Gaulle and Algeria, 1940-1960: From Mers El-Kébir to the Algiers Barracades [Sic].* London: Quartet, 1993.

Kloman, Erasmus H. *Assignment Algiers With the OSS in the Mediterranean Theater.* Annapolis, Md: Naval Institute Press, 2005.

Langer, William L. *Our Vichy Gamble.* New York: A.A. Knopf, 1947.

Moon, Tom. *This Grim and Savage Game: OSS and the Beginning of U.S. Covert Operations in World War II.* Cambridge, MA: Da Capo Press, 2000.

Murphy, Robert D. *Diplomat Among Warriors.* Garden City, N.Y.: Doubleday, 1964.

O'Donnell, Patrick K. *Operatives, Spies, and Saboteurs: The Unknown Story of the Men and Women of World War II's OSS.* New York: Free Press, 2004.

Perisco, Joseph E. *Roosevelt's Secret War.* New York: Random House, 2001.

Playfair, Ian Stanley Ord, C. J. C. Molony, F. C. Flynn, and T. P. Gleave. *The Mediterranean and Middle East. Vol.4, The Destruction of the Axis Forces in Africa.* History of the Second World War : United Kingdom military series. London: H.M.S.O., 1966.

Sayer, Ian, and Douglas Botting. *America's Secret Army The Untold Story of the Counter Intelligence Corps.* London: Grafton, 1989.

Słowikowski, Mieczysław Zygfryd, and John Herman. *In the Secret Service: The Lighting of the Torch.* London: Windrush Press, 1988.

Smith, R. Harris. *OSS: the Secret History of America's First Central Intelligence Agency.* Berkeley: University of California Press, 1972.

Tompkins, Peter. *The Murder of Admiral Darlan, A Study in Conspiracy.* New York: Simon and Schuster, 1965.

Troy, Thomas F. *Wild Bill and Intrepid Donovan, Stephenson, and the Origin of CIA.* New Haven: Yale University Press, 1996.

Vaughan, Hal. *FDR's Twelve Apostles: The Spies Who Paved the Way for the Invasion of North Africa.* Guilford, Conn: Lyons Press, 2006.

Government Documents

EE. UU. *War Report of the OSS.* New York: Walker, 1976.

Office of Strategic Services (OSS) : Organization and Functions. World War II Operational Documents.

U.S. Department of Defense. *Joint Publication 3-02.1 Joint Tactics, Techniques, and Procedures for Landing Force Operations.* Washington, DC: Government Printing Office, 2004.

US Department of the Army, Allied Force Headquarters, Office of Assistant Chief of Staff, G-2, 1943. *Intelligence Lessons from NORTH AFRICA OPERATION "TORCH".* Washington, DC.

US Department of the Army, Allied Force Headquarters, 1943. *Lessons of OPERATION TORCH.* Washington, DC.

www.ingramcontent.com/pod-product-compliance
Lightning Source LLC
Chambersburg PA
CBHW080312290526
45790CB00005B/2008